Open bull-jean gate
and conjure rises from the unbroken page into the soul—
which is surely deeper than it was before.

– Eisa Davis

Sharon is solar. She has a powerful central gravity; she gives off light and gives life a faithful reference—she writes from cause and her writing causes writing. Sharon's fierce honesty liberates delight and calls up compassion's responsibility. Noun by noun, diphthong and elision and swoop and nuance and sublimity at a time, she launches language that shares itself into an ambience of enlightenment. She reads us, and reading her we are brought up to our best selves. Her writing is material and complex enough to take on true love.

– Erik Ehn

Sharon Bridgforth's work is like breathing. It is both necessary and life-giving. I inhale the warmth and cool of her soulful southern lyricism and am able to exhale into bull-jean herself. Black/queer/masculine/butch/big-hearted/bull-dagger bull-jean. How wonderful to have this boldly crafted character guide us through the complicated terrain of love-making, love-conjuring, love's breaking, and love's lasting. And to witness her power become fully manifest in her relentless search for that romantic love. And how wonderful to have bull-jean back again, in her old age, to help guide us into healing, remembrance, and transition. Sharon Bridgforth's language channels in this new story as a gift from the ancestors: Dance, music, and rituals long forgotten. Love, a measure of what we leave behind. In the end, Bridgforth challenges us to consider if we've loved radically enough to become those loving ancestors we seek.

– Donnetta Lavinia Grays

53 SP 41
September 2022
Brooklyn, NY

*bull-jean & dem/dey back*
© Sharon Bridgforth 2022
53rdstatepress.org

ISBN Number: 978-1737025566
Library of Congress Number: 2022942547

Book design: Kate Kremer
Cover design: vind datter

Printed on recycled paper in the United States of America.

*bull-jean & dem/dey back* is made possible by the New York State Council on the Arts with the support of the Office of the Governor and the New York State Legislature.

# bull-jean & dem/dey back

by sharon bridgforth

53rd state press
brooklyn, ny

I dedicate this book to Lisa C. Moore. Mutha of the houze of RedBone Press...may all the Divine labor/Vision/laughter/power and Love that you have so generously poured into me/bull-jean/and all your chil'ren return to you a hundred fold as Blessings.

Let the good times roll/yeah...

## contents

## preface

I began writing *the bull-jean stories* in the '90s after the last of my elders on my mom's side passed. I wanted to hear their voices again. So I started writing in ways that awakened their raucous, holy, tender, Loving, self-determining Spirits in me. In doing this I developed a writing practice based in listening/feeling and receiving with my essence. bull-jean carried me into my writer's voice. She carried me to my blues-based/theatrical jazz self. She exposed—and helped me release—my unhealthy Method-writing tendencies, and she is the reason I grew through some serious Life issues.

Now, in 2022, as I face my mother's mortality, as we all grieve and bear witness to loss, as this dysfunctional world shows its nasty ass, and as the truths that my queer Black Ancestors have long been reckoning with/turn this mutha outt … bull-jean has returned. This time she is coming with her posse of southern-Black-butch-sheroes, ole folk/tricksters, dat Black Mermaid Man Lady (who first appeared in my show that premiered in 2018) and children that fly. bull-jean and dem here to root the Narrator in Love. To ensure that the Narrator knows how to expand their capacity to hold/and feel everything that this time in Life is Offering. Dey here … in all their queer-splendored, many-gendered Black forms from all sides of the veil to wake us—Open/Free.

1998

i am a child of the motown era/raised on aretha franklin, bobby blue bland, bb king/grits, greens and smothered porkchops. my mother migrated west (the promised land) but carried her southern sensibilities with her: we listened to gospel music on sundays (in lieu of church service); revered the dead; and recognized music, food, dancing, telling tales and laughing as a way to heal/and pray.

in the tradition of my upbringing, *the bull-jean stories* are performance stories/part of, not separate from, Life and Ancestral Spirits. i see *the bull-jean stories* as a blues quilt/each story an individual composition that speaks on survival and love/together creating a complete picture of one wo'mn's journey through many Life-times learning emotional and Spiritual balance. bull-jean rarely speaks but when she does/it is most often in the form of poetry    the language of the Heart.

with *the bull-jean stories* i wanted to celebrate the rural/southern working-class Black bulldaggas/who were aunty-mamma-sister-friend/pillars of the church    always been

a working part of our community/giving fierce Love with fineness. the songs of my childhood/the laughter/the gift of tale-telling/the food that my elders gave me are integral parts of who i am. though i can't dictate their particular words i do understand that the voice of *the bull-jean stories* belongs to them. these are the stories they didn't tell me    the ones i needed most. bull-jean is the butch/southern/poet/warrior wo'mn hero i wish i'd known.

i hope you enjoy this dance/this taste of creating-remembering with me...

– Sharon Bridgforth

# the bull-jean stories

1998

bull-jean first appeared in 1993 in *lovve/rituals & rage* performed by The root wy'mn Theatre Company—Sharon Bridgforth: founder, writer, artistic director; company members: Anoa Monsho, Sonja Parks, Arriama Matlock-Abdullah, and Kaci Fannin; company manager: Lori D. Wilson.

In 2010 Q-roc Ragsdale received support from the National Performance Network Creation Fund, with support from the South Dallas Cultural Center and Diverseworks Art Space, to create a multimedia adaptation of *the bull-jean stories*.

The Drama League DirectorFest produced *the bull-jean stories* in 2021:

Signe V. Harriday – director
Ameerah Briggs – performer
Chris De Camillis – stage manager
X Casting/Victor Vazquez, CSA – casting director
Aimee K. Bryant – vocal consultant
Michael Mueller, JC Quiroz Vizhnay, Ben Starkman – camera operators

*the bull-jean stories* will be produced by Pillsbury House + Theatre in 2022/2023:

Signe V. Harriday – director
Elizabeth R. MacNally – production manager

## opening | mary anne adams

*bull-jean & dem/dey back* is the magical potion we've been waiting for: Sharon Bridgforth's work allows me to be my Black deep southern lesbian self. Because Bridgforth's performance stories are so authentic and multi-layered, we find out not only who her characters are, but who we are. And this is transformative.

On a Thursday night in 1999 when Bridgforth began reading from *the bull-jean stories* at Charis Bookstore in Atlanta, Georgia, the hairs on my arms stood on end. The characters that she so eloquently brought to life immediately took me back to the rolling hills of north Mississippi where I came of age in the '60s and '70s. I wondered how Bridgforth knew the unmarried Black women of my childhood. The women in Freedman's Town that lived in tandem, the single women everyone whispered about in low tones, whom they sometimes named old maid and spinster, but mostly bull-dykes and bull-daggers. These women who settled comfortably in their own skin wearing shapeless dresses, scandalous britches, and unshaved legs in brogans. How had Bridgforth so intimately captured the everyday lives of these women who taught secondary school and Bible classes, laughed long and hard, and, much like bull-jean sometimes sought love in all the wrong places. I was shook that night at Charis Bookstore—I loved those women of my youth because they were different, they were outcasts, they were sister outsiders, and I was too.

Bridgforth dared to write outside the lines with *the bull-jean stories*. She gave us a lyrical trove that held us spell-bound, and wove a magical tale of the rural south, unapologetic same-sex attraction and bad-ass Black women who lived by the rules they made. I sat there that Thursday night desperately longing to be like bull-jean when I grew up. I wanted to live in the world that Bridgforth so skillfully conjured up through her blend of spirit, vision, memory, and memoir. Reading *the bull-jean stories* was exquisite, but listening to the audio version and witnessing a bull-jean performance was like eating chitterlings with hot sauce on white bread at a Mississippi juke joint, sitting between your mamma's knees while she cornrowed your hair, and hiding your giggle behind the church fan when the Deacon fell asleep once again. The book and CD accompanied my friends and me on many road trips and provided countless hours of affirmation and empowerment.

In 2017, I had lunch with Bridgforth in San Francisco and casually inquired about bull-jean's whereabouts. In the 20-plus years since *the bull -jean stories*, there have been major events in the US: 9/11, the Iraq War, Hurricane Katrina, the first Black president, the legalization of same-sex marriage, school and church shootings, the Affordable Care Act, the first Black woman vice-president, and Supreme Court Justice, and the Covid-19 pandemic. bull jean is the voice, the teacher, the sage, the elder we need to help us grow beyond what we have so far dared to imagine.

Bridgforth is a gifted story-teller, and in *bull-jean & dem/dey back*, she conjures up a world that is at once familiar and new. bull-jean's old friends will be warmed by her presence and new readers will dive into her complexities and simplicities, vulnerabilities and bad-assness.

> – Mary Anne Adams
> Founder & Executive Director, ZAMI NOBLA—
> National Organization of Black Lesbians on Aging

**chapter I.**

## bull-jean & sassy b. gonn

there go bull-jean and she aunty     sassy b. gonn.
ever wednesday/twice on sundays
bull-jean go git she aunty     walk to the sto.
sassy old as dirt/cain't hear/don't memember today/done
drank she near-blind ass half to hell     and bull-jean
Lovve her/go git she aunty
ever wednesday
twice on sundays
walk to the sto.

sassy be talking loud enough to disturb the dead
say
*lawd/baby*
*you walks lik yo*
*bloods is on you     all-blacker in the face/eyes sunked/and*
*jes look at you*

*you been fuckn!*

*i done tole you/you cain't be fuckn ten days befo yo bloods!*

yessuh
ole sassy liable to say anythang.
*secret is*
*to dress warm*

*cause if you gits a cold in yo cock/it'll go straight to yo head      kill you fo*
*time.*

na/one wednesday sassy got sick clear through sunday      in bed.
bull-jean had to call ole doc benson who was breathing in sassy's face
wid him eye-light when she came to

lawd

that hefa cain't run no furtha than she can piss/but i declare
she quick      reached under that bed
whipped up she shooter/had that man pent to the wall fo he could take
him next breath. sassy say
*you touch me/i'll kill yo soul*
*and dare yo Spirit to rise*
      she done had a flash-back
*i'll tare yo Heart out*
*and spit-in-the-middle.*

bull-jean in the back jesa hollering
**aunt-mamma/aunt-mamma**
**give me the gun aunt-mamma!**
sassy say
*since when you start coming cross the tracks.*
*you wouldn't come ova here when my baby came twisted out the womb*
*you wouldn't come*
*when them hooded beasts burned the skin offa my man/and*
*gottdamn      you didn't come when they snatched my sister-split she limbs*
*taking turns on her back      i figa/you got enough blood on yo hands*

*from  no-care*
*i ain't giving you nonna mines.*

parently
sassy done forgot she useta forgave the white peoples
*you betta git on away from we!*

well

ventually/bull-jean got the gun from she aunty.
na/sassy add that story to the other six she tell ova
and ova
cept she don't memember being sick      some how
it all change to how she likta kill a man trying to save bull-jean.

yessuh

they be walking
bull-jean and she aunty
ever na and again
sassy look up      lik she seeing bull-jean fo the first time-the-day
say
*hey baby*
*when you join up?*

sassy smile/take bull-jean's face
cup-in-both-hands
look the gurl in the eyes
say

*you know/you always was*
*my favorite     we*
*cut from the same rug/we.*
bull-jean smile/say
**yes ma'am.**

they walk on
hand-n-hand
stroll down the way
ever wednesday
twice on sundays
when bull-jean go git she aunty
sassy b. gonn     walk to the sto.

## bull-jean slipn in

ever day
5am
deacon willie/clara's man
go git him
supplies     umph
everbody know
nappy love
be the one filling him sack.

every day
5am
deacon willie/clara's man
slip out     bull-jean
slip in
     clara git her supplies too.

bull-jean say
**one GOOD thirty minutes**
**lasts a Life-time**
umph bull-jean and clara
got mo Life-times than a cat's times infinity     i know
cause i been watching them bout that long.
     not that i'm nosey or nuthn/cause
     i got business of my own you see/but
every day
5:30am

bull-jean slip out
look ruffled/smile dusty
eyes rolled     tongue damn near wagging
*close yo mouth gurl* i say
she don't hear
jes float on down the way.

one morning
5:30am
i jes snatch her on in sit down/talk right-in-her-face
*bull-jean when you gonn smell the coffee*
*that gal is married!* i said
blam/slam her some coffee so strong it don't move in the cup.
bull-jean say
**i been giving away tastes**
**piece by piece/samples**
**of my Heart/i**
**been giving for free     all my Life**
**it's almost gonn/my Heart**
**all i really want**
**is a kind word**
**and a smile**

**and that wo'mn is kind**
**and she Lovves me     and**
**it don't matter if it's thirty minutes a day**
**or ONCE in the next Life**
**i'll go git her/smile**

**whenever she'll let me**
**have it!**

bull-jean go back to looking drifty.
umph/seem to me they be doing more than smiling
ova there.

then one day
5am
deacon willie/clara's man
didn't slip out
but bull-jean slipped in
shiit
i got my gun
figured all hell would break loose ova there
and spread my way
i waited
   and
      waited

5:05am
deacon willie/clara's man come out
tail dragging
sit on the porch holding him head
till 5:30am
bull-jean come out the FRONT door
and nodd him good-bye

struttn!

na/everbody know
the deacon was doing nappy love
but it turned out
deacon willie/clara's man
also been squeezing frosty jackson's onions/and frosty got
mo sugga in him shorts than the sto got sacks to hold it in
    so i guess that make the deacon
    semi-sweet.
bull-jean tole ole deacon
unless he want her to tell the wind/he better
go git some money from him honey
cause he was moving out
and she was moving in!

ain't no mo
slipn in/or out
ova there.
all i see is bull-jean and clara floating round
smiling.

ever na and then they come ova
sit wid me    looking drifty.
i give em some of my strong-ass-coffee
but they don't seem to smell it

and that makes me
smile.

## bull-jean & that wo'mn

cleandra marie la beau
say she lik the way i
tickle her spot/say
folk keepa fiddling round but cain't seem to
find it/lik
i can      she
take my hand      place it on her Heart/say
*that's*
*my spot*
*bull-jean/and since you touch it so sweet*
*i'm gonn let you see what else of mine*
*you can find to tickle ...*

oh/i'm so in Lovve      till
i'm sick/jes
hurt
all ova
body
   ache
mind
   sore
Heart
   hurt/jes
hurt

and it all began when i looked in the eyes of THAT WO'MN.

na/i's a wo'mn
whats Lovved many wy'mns.
me/they call bull-dog-jean     i say
thats cause i works lik somekinda ole dog trying to git a bone or two
they say it's cause i be sniffing after wy'mns
down-low/begging and thangs

whatever.

one day
i was sitting in my yard
telling tales and dranking wid my pal lou     when
i thought i heard a rustling
   i didn't look up cause the dogs was jes
   laying-round-not-saying-a-thang
   usually they barks at everythang
cluding me
so i jes kepa-dranking and telling
till i heard a voice
         *hello*
well i lik to fell ova in the petunias
sounded lik heaven to me
i looked round and lawdy-mercy what i have to do that fo/na
i know you done heard this befo
but this wo'mn is here to testify:  **DON'T MESS WID THEM
FULL-GROWN/FULL-FLEDGE/SHO-NUFF-HOT-BUTT
WY'MNS!**
they'll drop a spell on you quicker'n you can say please

chile
i looked up and SHE caught me
wid her eyes     i ain't got loose yet.

fo the longest i didn't even see the rest of her
so lost in them eyes/deep
clear/flickering brown/Spirit-talking eyes
    take me na lawd     i said
    fo one moment in them eyes and i done lived full-in-yo glory
cain't recall much was said right away
too busy staring in them eyes.
fo the longest i didn't even see the rest of her

then i saw lips/full and quick to smile
    loose me lawd/git me out her spell
    i said     mouth watering/i thought
bet she sho know how to do some good Lovvn/lips so fine and all.
fo the longest i didn't even see the rest of her

then i looked on down and saw nipples lunging/hips ready to roll
sweet glory in the morning
    i'm done seen an angel
    in the form of flesh
thats when i gave up the ghost
jes said
here
fo i know'd SHE was the kinda wo'mn make you want to give it up/
say

baby
  take  me
    take all i got
      take all i'll ever git
       tell me
         what you want gal
here
i'll give it jes to see you smile.

fate were standing before me
giving me a big brown hello.

and sho-nuff
i done spent all the rest of my days
tickling a permanent smile on that wo'mn's face.

## bull-jean & trouble

i knew
trouble had done left     when i saw bull-jean sitting at the b.y.o. wid
jucey la bloom
i knew
trouble was gonn

cause jucey don't drank
and bull-jean don't hang
lessn some wo'mn done broke she Heart/and baby
bull-jean musta sho-nuff been hurting
cause jucey had done drank the fat part of a rat's ass jigg'd.
you see bull-jean and jucey la bloom
friends from last-Life/they so close
they feel one-the-other's pain
jucey say
*i think*
*i'll begin Life again     come back*
*a dog/cock my leg or squat     bow-wow-mafucka*
*folk gonn haveta deal wid MY shit*
*next time round*
yessuh/they business jes skooch-ova to my table
      cause you know i ain't a nosey-wo'mn.
jucey say
*she ain't nuthn but a periodic-ho     ain't even got sense nuff to charge*
*on a regular basis*
bull-jean sit

holding she head
low to the table     stream-a-tears
rolling down the left side she face/her
don't bat a eye/nor make sound.
jucey on the other hand
jesa howling/rocking backwards and forwards/eyes rolling
*why/bull-jean/why you git we in this mess gurl*
*why?*
bull-jean raise up
say
**trouble/came in**
**stood to the side**
  **made me**
    **sense her first**
**russling skirt/jiggling jewelry/clicking**
**heels     trouble/came in**
**smelt lik sunshine     lik**
**freedom on a bed of posies/trouble**
**made me want her**
**befo i ever saw her face     she**
**entered my Heart**
**and held me/trouble**
**came in     ass popping**
**from side to side**
**she carried me across the room in her gaze/i**
**got lost**
**haven't found my way back**
**from trouble/she holds me**

in her smile     i fit
between the moist on her lips/i
fit between her ears/i fit
in the middle of her intent/i fit
at the end of her fingers
i fit
in the pressure of her voice/her
heat as it lifts me/at the tip
of her thoughts as they extend themselves/wid
the extent of her desire/i
fit     i done laid down wid trouble/and
cain't
git
up!

trouble came in
  stood to the side
    and took me
home.

jucey la bloom
jes hugged she head and she bottle
and cried.

## bull-jean's elements of lovve

you are Earth     i am Ocean
let me
cast my waters
up on
yo sho.
you are Sun
i is Moon/moving
to envelop
the distance
from out
our way.

you are Fire     i am Wind
oh/how i wants to
blow yo flame!

na see/that gurl
ain't got no sense.
be out under
sugga-sweet's
window     every
friday/come Moon-up
moaning

i will dance wid you through time
endure all thangs in yo embrace

**smiling**
**as Life brings us closer**

**if this is not my destiny/then**
**i must Live again      because**
**nuthn**
**in this world**
**can keep me from you**
**   not even death ...**

umph/her gonn die alright
sugga gonn
ignore
the Life outta she.

cain't tell bull-jean that
though/she say
her and sugga Souls married last-Life/ain't
done yet

**there are no words**
**fo some thangs      lik**
**the way my eyes**
**delight in yo's**
**lik**
**the sweetness of closen you      the**
**smell of yo breath in mine/yo**
**softness filling me/on you knowing**

us full      there
are no words
for some thangs
lik
the way you move me/yo
voice touching my Heart/lik
feeling
beyond-feeling/there
are
no words for
what you mean
to me/there
are
no
words      won't
you
let
me
make expression
for the thangs
language won't
let
me
say
   gal?

i sits out wid my cup
ever

friday/come Moon-up     listen to they.
na/far as i can make-out
bull-jean ain't made-out yet.
sugga won't let her in the house/and
won't come out     jes
lean from the window a spell
then shut the shade

shiit

some nights
all bull-jean
can get out is a croon'n

**lawd/lawd/lawd**
**oh my**
**lawd/lawd/lawd**
**oh lawd**

it take bugga to tell it though
bugga is sugga's gran-aunty on she daddy's side who be my aunt butta's
ex-husband/uncle chain's second-wife's sista
anyway
bugga-sweet
counsel wid bull-jean
say
*na/i*
*done had*

*enough*
*pussaay*
*to last till i returns*

*you*
*on the other hand*
*needs*
*some gurl*

*i don't know*
*what*
*you done-done*
*to that gal last-Life*
*but i don't reckon she near-fixnta*
*let you Lovve her this one*

*so go on wid yo-self!*

na/first off
look lik bugga ain't had enougha nuthn
cause i seen nuckie-little
crawling out she window
jes last week
looking lik that ole no-tooth-hefa done ju-ju she draws
   course i got better thangs to do
   than watch the goings on at the sweet house
   but i jes cain't stand to see
   po bull-jean

suffering so
i done tried to git her to come
ova here fo tea
steada ova there
fo misery

anyway

bugga say
*go on*
*git you one them*
*seasoned-suzzies/a*
*big-bettye or a*
*tight-tammye.*
*you needs*
*a ready ripe-wrapped/done-done-it wo'mn.*
*and if you feels*
*anythang*
*what resemble Lovve*

*RUN!!!*

*cause you know*
*you cain't handle it/be*
*ova here all looped up*
*and thangs.*

bull-jean
let that nine-Life cat

jesa-keepa-talking
    till nuckie-little come by
    whistle bugga to the bushes.

bull-jean sit there
looking
con-fused
till
up come the shade
and out the window
stick sugga she head

bull-jean say
**sugga**
**all i want to do**
**is give yo thoughts affection**
  **soothe yo feelings wid kindness**
    **and give yo dreams some Lovvn.**
**i won't be trying to touch**
**nuthn but friendship**
**if thats all you want**
**to give me.**

chile

the shade
neva went down
that night.

next thang i know
bull-jean
IN THE HOUSE WID SUGGA
friday/come Moon-up/stay till Moon-down.

all i hear is laughter/the
smell of
chicken
sizzln

and
the sound of bugga running
through the bushes
cause she cain't break loose the spell
she put on nuckie-little!

## bull-jean & next-life/blues

this is the story of
Lovve ain't enough

it's about
fear and saddness/and
next-Life
blues

this

is the story of
one wo'mn's
struggle to ungrip
she Soul
from misery...

na/it all
began
befo i know      and it all
ended
full-Moon day/some time
ago/middla
safirra louise goode's
wedding.

safirra      the reverend peter goode sr.'s

only
gurl/sweet
as she is
rotten.
got a slow grin/a
ripe ass
and enough
of the devil in her
to drive any good fool
madd.

her    promised to
sampson tucka johnson/the reverend
e.m. johnson's
youngest/owner of
tucka's joint
cross the county line.

the two reverends figa
between they
two sinning off-spring
at least one God fearing child
oughts to be got.

safirra figa she
make her daddy happy
and
enjoy tucka's fast life and long money/tucka

figa he get
some good help
and free lovvn.

so it was on

the biggest
two-preacha-four-choir-twelve-deacon
high rolling broom-jump
of all time.

only thang
bout it
safirra     bull-jean's wo'mn!
hell
everbody
know it
safirra
ain't nuthn but two-sided/walk
ever whicha way/lik she gots to have it all     mens
in the street/bull-jean
in the sheets/jes
all-of-it

po bull-jean.
spoil that wo'mn/jes lik the gurl daddy     let she have her way
all the time

but ever body

know safirra
done gonn too far
this time
tole bull-jean
*baby/if you Lovves me*
*lik you say you do*
*you gots to want to*
*share in this most important*
*event in my life*
say
*after all*
*my Heart*
*belongs to*
*you/you*
*the one*
*i really*
*Lovves/always*
*will find a way*
*to get to you*
*mamma.*

umph

chile
folk was all up in that church house
come broom-jump time/jes
packed     fanning and showing out/waiting and all/they was up in
there/um-hmm

anyway

everthang
was jes-beautiful

till the reverend e.m. ask
*do anyone here*
*have cause to object*
*to this matrimonial binding*
*of god's choosing?*

bull-jean
stood
up
   had on she best suit/pressed and all
say
**looka here**
**this**
**ain't no binding/and it**
**sho ain't none of God's choosing     i**
**the one put on this earth**
**to walk wid that wo'mn and/i**
**the one oughta be up there wid her na/so**
**yessuh**
**mr. reverend preacha man**
**i take the right**
**to make objection**
**to this**

lie-befo God.

SAFIRRA

you my
biscuits and gravy

the amen
at the end of my prayers     you
my perfumed hallelujah
     sweet chariot stop and let me ride/you
my southern comfort
my gi-tar
stroking
all night
cradling the scent of you/are
my memories/you are
all the wy'mn i have
ever
Lovved     my
last-Life-Lovve
come back/my
new Moon
dancing across a cool stream
you
are settled
in the depths of me

**and no matter where you go**
**who you wid**
**or what you do**
**you**

**is**

**MINES!!!**

chile

you coulda heard
a mouse fart.
cept ole
conchita la fraud
and she sista weewee
had they black asses
giggling in the back of the church/slurping and
fussing ova they sack drank
    at po bull-jean's most serious moment

anyway

bull-jean
jes stand there
say
**saddness/settle in the bones**
**you know    it rots**
**the will and puts out**

the fires of Life
you gonn be sad
wo'mn
cause i'm fixnta
be gonn
and i ain't
gonn be dead.

bull-jean
look safirra
in the eye/real hard
say
i may not
be able to promise
you fancy rangs
and furs and thangs
but i guarantee
that when we kiss
you'll hear the Angels sang      and
if that ain't enough
to fill yo Life wid joy
and comfort

i
release
you
na
Lovve.

her
turn and walk out.

safirra pass out
boom!
all up in the sanctuary
lik somebody done snipped she cord-a-Life.
ain't
been the same since

butt donn dropped
eyes dull/even
the devil done left her      she
sanctified na
jump and holla
everwhere
cept in bed      i hear she
neva do help tucka neitha

anyway

bull-jean
she bitta.
sit round
sangn the same
sorryass thang all the time
**Lovve**
**will kill you**

**break yo Heart**
**in two**

**say/Lovve**
**will kill you**

**break yo Heart**
**in two**

**i'm so**
**sick of Lovve**

**i don't know**
**what to do.**

i done tried to tole her
*see/yo mind and yo mouth*
*left the wo'mn      but*
*yo soul*
*still gripped round that ass/clangn*
*on fo dear life*

*you best pry it free*
*fo you be stuck wid that gurl fo all time.*
her no hear me/naw
too busy wadding in bittaness

**Lovve**
**will kill you**

break yo Heart
in two

i'm so
sick of Lovve
i don't know
what to do.

## bull-jean & the power of no mo

there is so much
silence
widout you.

it's the hardest thang    i'll
never get used to/this
silence widout you
i am trapped
by my own space/my
memory remains locked
in your voice    forcing
me to grieve the days
of our discontent.

silence holds me na
and keeps me
restless
in the absence
of you.

useta be
sweet
thoughtful minded
 helpful handed
  empathy actioned    useta
wouldn't mind/give

my last smile
to my wo'mn-useta all
talk about how sweet i be

well

i
ain't sweet
no mo     put sweet out
myself
sweet
ain't got me
nuthn
but left.
i done decided
no mo

no mo
sleeping wid sorrow in
a empty bed     no mo
longing what cain't
be filled/no mo
yo-last-visit-ghost give
me haint'd Heart/cain't
get drunk enough mind scarred     i
ain't chasing the blues
no mo.

it's time
i
settle down
wid me!

## bull-jean is b.j. la rue

i na know      the secret of
b.j. la rue.

b.j.
live what you call a
sportn life    sports
different wy'mns/all the time
             till ole mary butte come long/neva-left.
b.j.
sang somewhere uptown
leave round dinner
come back at lunch    tuesday
thru sunday
             till ole mary butte come long.
b.j.
pressed/always
crisp    wear black
short sleeve shirt show
how hard the meat packed/bagged
pants belted up
winged out-fresh shined shoes
skin
greased
hair
low
 slick

    b.j. be sportn

i been trying to find out

                where that club is so i can

              go/get me some     sangn-to

anyway

somethang bout b.j. have always twitched my mind

couldn't figure zackly what it were

then it come to me


b.j. la rue                  BULL-DOG-JEAN


yessuh!

see

back home

my mamma's sista live next to the dutrey house by the crawfish hole ova

to the la rue's.     the la rue boys/hittn-stick/strang-finga/song/and

horn-head

is musical

hittn-stick boy tootie/marry ms. nu-moon gurl/had too many babies/

sent the oldest to

they city sista     i thankn

i ain't neva seen the child

till i heard b.j. sangn

                    **i'd lik to be**

                    **the coffee in yo cup**

                    **the first thang**

                    **you put your lips on**

                    **each day**

**i'd lik to be**
**the coffee in yo cup**
**what you grind**
**at night**
**to get on your way**

her trying to get ole mary butte to let her back in the house
sound jes lik she daddy tootie/ms. nu-moon gurl man
i said
*baby/you ain't got to stand in that yard/sangn fo suppa/i gots plentya food*
*right*
*here*

anyway
parently the club owners twist off she name      make more money
letting the mens think her a man-sangn-man-sorrows

tell you what

them wy'mn's know her a she
      be all flocked round
i hearing she don't even hardly try to make no business wid em
jes hug up/talk/have tea      listen to they
      then ole mary butte come long/tore that playhouse down!
i said/jes tell me why you had to invite mary stay.
bull-jean say
**it was the way she smiled at me/wid her eyes**
**pouty lips/parted**
**deep breath laugh/the**

**Sun resting on her neck**
**head back**
**a little to the side      it was**
**the way one strap**
**fell slightly off her shoulder**
**breasts sitting playful**
**waist**
**curvn/hips**
**turned in seat**
**jes a bit.**
**it was the way she knew me**
**wid her smile**
**that told me**
**this wo'mn was home.**

umph.

anyway
bull-jean
still sporty-dress in black-packaged hard/cept na
go uptown/after dinner
be home by dusk      tuesday thru saturday
              ole mary make she go to church
              ha!

                          **let me**
                          **be the coffee in yo cup**
                          **hold me close/smell**
                          **your memories**

wake

black/wid
a little sugar
made to fit your taste
stir and sip me slow
don't let none go to waste

i need to be yo coffee baby
long as you want your cup filled up/i'd
lik to be the coffee/baby
waiting for you    in yo cup.

## bull-jean got read

they got read    not red lik the color but read lik
she can read music therefo she well
read

um hmm

they got read/bull-jean gonn get her na.
read overto the jailhouse hollern
*i'ma good mafuckn citizen/why you got me chaindup lik this    mafuckas*
if read name wasn't read it'd be mafucka cause she mafucks us to death
round here.
her niece babygurl gets it the most though/when every sunday after
church babygurl holds reads licka hostage/read chase babygurl down the
street *give me my mafuckn bottle back*
*mafucka*
i don't know why read bother run/gonn get a bottle by friday when
she sang her drunk ass round town fo dranks.

bull-jean useta run wid read    hard
but since babett left
bull-jean don't drank no mo/don't run none
babett
    babett johnson/not babett dushard/the dushards is my relation/the
    johnsons belong to tufus and them-on they daddy's aunty's husband
    side/which is why i know all this cause my cousin pooky
    married tufus uncle brother

um hmm

bull-jean still trying to get babett back

**talk to me**
**tell me**
**what you want**
**i'd lik to know/whats**
**on your mind     whats**
**going on inside you/baby**
**talk to me**
**please**
**respond…**

um hmm

bull-jean and read useta start friday hit the road/hit every club crossing
three county lines     by sunday morning be back at the country mile
propped
for the late last show.
make babett stay home wait/while she badd ass ack-out
all ova everwhere.
but since babett left
bull-jean walk away from her bottle and her bad ackn
**my Heart hurts**
**from reaching**
**for you/you're not here**
**i need to**

**see your smile**
**smell you/have your laughter**
**dear     i am so lonely**
**say you'll see me**
**just once more**

**i thirst for you.**
**quench me quick/give me**
**your skin/touch me**
**let me turn to you**
**and sleep.**

baby/babett done broke that wo'mn down.

see/babett from what you calls
a musical family
the daddy's-daddy pass it     they all play some form of instrument
some in a classical way some/honky-tonk but they all plays
thats how babett met bull-jean/cause read
was taking lesson from babett daddy
bull-jean tag along cause practice on friday right befo getround time.
well
Lovve is nice and all but babett wasn't no messround gurl/had thangs to
do songs to play/couldn't do nuthn
wid all the mess bull-jean kept round.

**i always hoped to hold you**
**to treasure you/i meant to**

**be kind
and thoughtful and clear     i wanted to
never leave
never take you for granted/to honor
each moment
i intended
to love you well.**

shiit     babett gonn/and
thankyoujesus heavenly saints angels and holy ancestors     bull-jean
don't drink no mo!
read
on the other hand done loss her family/fine clothes/pocket change
and her front teef     still dranking
bull-jean gonn get her na
neva
get babett back though/cause
sometimes you cain't get back what a ass done loss following a sick mind

um hmm/yeah.

## bull-jean at big briggette's

the room was full    we
carried disappointment heavily/though
loudly we laughed the world out our heads/for
jes a moment
we found ease/being Coloured
in america/it was our day of rest
late friday till mid-sunday
at club seeyaround    late
friday till mid-sunday

bull-jean was there.
at her table in the corner in the front
  she waited
    lik everbody else
      cept bull-jean wasn't gripped on a drank
      lik some of us/no
      cause drank
      done already made her dead
      and crazy/well but
      thats a whole nutha story/yeah.
then it happened
serafine agata santiago showed herself on stage

her don't jes walk out
she appear
wavy black-brown/thick hipped/curvy tasty/fiiine

chocolate

>> a collection of rhythms/kept-sounds
>> body released variations of layers of
>> syncopated memories from
>> many times back

feet-da  dadada  da hips-swish swish dip and swirl head-turn/and stare
and turn/stare and turn fingers-snappn clap clap snap snappn pouch
poutn lips smile
smile
all light ray-out in one blink.


her don't jes walk out/she vision forth
and when she unleash that voice
all hell break loose/yeah     the peoples jes lose they mind

> i grab my zin-zin and pray
> cause i know her done worked up a juju long befo
> she open her mouth/sang
> well but thats a whole nutha story/yeah

>> *meet me when the leaves change*
>> *meet me when the boatbell clang*
>>
>> *say/meet me when the leaves change*
>> *meet me when the boatbell clang*
>>
>> *i'ma take you down the river*
>> *gonn make you holla/make you sang*

*say/meet me baby*
*jes want you to come half-way*

*say/meet me baby*
*gonn show you what words cain't neva say*

na/only fools
       and strangers
even thank bout ackn-out in club seeyaround
cause
the proprietress       big briggette
will not only kick yo ass/she will
hunt you down-tare yo home to the ground
then tell yo mamma.

              you ask for it/if you ack-out in
              big briggette's place/yeah
it is said she can suck all the air out the room/use it
to knock the head off yo body       in one blow
              well but you know
              thats a whole nutha story/yeah!

na/we all know
everbody ack-a-fool
sometime

baby
it musta been fool's nite out at club seeyaround that nite/cause
wasn't a stranger in site.

na/historical fact is
we done most often fought onetheother because
somebody's somebody thought they somebody
done done it wid somebody else/yeah

well
serafine sangn

> *somethangs gota hold of me*
> *i cain't let go*
>
> *somethangs gota hold of me*
> *the only thang i know*
> *is i want to do what we said*
> *we wasn't gonn do no mo*
>
> *say/i want to do what we did*
> *lik we done it befo*

lil red lilly musta thought her tufus thought serafine
was sangn to her/yeah/cause
bam    lilly knock ole tufus upside her head right there
front center table
papa ann got up out her seat from back the room
            thats when i knew some shit was fixn to happen
everbody but tufus know lil red lilly is papa ann's midnight delight
don't lik to see lil lilly upset    came up
front center table
broke a bottle of some good licka on tufus head

big briggette stood up
everbody stopped breathing/jes
        stopped

see/big briggette don't walk/no
she re-arrange the room getting from place to place
her reach ova toss ole tufus clear out the club/then step out after she

tufus mamma was there went on out too/madd cause
tufus done pause our good-got-damn-day of rest
see/some time a fool jes sitting round
        being theyselves is enough to cause trouble

well/we all get back to breathing
serafine
start up again/sangn beaming right into bull-jean's eyes/putting a work
on bull-jeans grinning ass foreal

        well but thats a whole nutha story/yeah.

## bull-jean & mina stay

i from da swamp.  my fo-matha
snap two man neck/run free ta swamp people/we
long time from here
da ship ova stop at island
trade fo-matha man
fo wata    fo-fatha kill/oh six    seven
fin freedom too.
since dat time we people go from island ta swamp
be wid one da otha

dats how mina git here/she island gurl sent
by my uncle elias firs born daughta chile/when she small small
she not my baybay    but is.

on dis day    mina sit
mumble mumble/suck teef    her madd at bull-jean.
bull-jean sit/sit no talk    stuck
done let so many wrong-words out cain't fin da right ones no mo.
i been tole bull-jean *git on-way gurrl*
*come back when you got some right words.*
bull-jean tuck'd tail leave come back leave come back go ta she
gran-granny's/tryn think
find some right words fo mina
still on dis day sit sit no talk/words stuck in mouth.

so useta havn she way bull-jean is

all da time all da wy'mns give her everthang
cept stay     bull-jean use dat as cause ta
ack-out no git long no work it out     no stay.
i telln her
problem is
you been barkn at da wrong tree     if you know
you lookn at a cat
why you spect it ack lik a dog
a cat-is a cat/ain't nuthn but
a cat     why you barkn at it cause it ain't a dog/you da dog gurrl!

bull-jean want mina stay mus talk no-bark no ack-out
cause mina see a barkn dog/move on
bull-jean cain't capture mina/mina got ta want come stay.
mina say

> *why you trying to call me yo wife bull-jean*
> *wife*
> *what do that mean anyway?*
> *i been called wife befo*
> *turned my whole Life ova to the concept/to*
> *obey to have foever till death     i done*
> *that/already died once*
> *wasting prayers on makebelieve/rose*
> *up from a bed of lies/untended*
> *wilted and left     woke up robbed*
> *of precious time and sweet joy*

> *look lik     wife*

*is a word folk use when they want*
*license to control you     if you trying*
*to claim me bull-jean/jes call me yo wo'mn*
*that's what i am*
*a wo'mn*
*complete*
*wid or widout you     i'll be*
*yours/long as its right*
*but i need you to tell me*
*what you want/exactly what*
*you asking me     cause*
*wife*
*ain't saying nuthn right/in my mind!*

umph/dey go bak ta it
bull-jean standn/wid a badd case of da tongue tied
mina sitn     wid da sour con cepts
mumble mumble suck teef
     i jes tryn ta blend wid da wood
     cain't go in da houze not know
sit sit mumble stand
silent
silent/blend
umph
dey givn me da tight Heart

den looka
bull-jean come foward     on knees ta mina

hold hands/take eyes say
mina tisono
i bull-dog-jean
am asking you to be my wo'mn
whole and complete     in all essence
i want to make this journey/this Life
wid you     i want to wake
to the smell of your hair/the taste
of your neck     each morning/i
want you curled into me so i can
turn you open/to the
light of your eyes

i want to offer all the tenderness
and consideration i am capable
of/and more     gently/i want
to treasure tomorrows possibilities wid you
exchange dreams/walk through the challenges
of the day/share minds wid you
mina i want to pray     in the
curve of your hips the turn of your
lips the wet of your kiss/i want
to praise God for the Blessing of you.

as long as it's right
i want you to
stay
be who you are wid fierceness

**be honest wid me**
**and see me when you look**

**that is what i want/that's**
**what i am asking      be**
**my wo'mn mina**

bull-jean breathe those last words into mina
**be my wo'mn mina**
three times
and three times mina breathe back
*i'm yo wo'mn bull-jean*
*be mine*

yeah/i go in da houze na wid a
strong Heart knowin da future
done finally laid down wid Lovve...

## bull-jean's aunt tilly

*na/i shoots mafuckas.*
*yessuh    run through*
*my yard    crawlout.*
*shiitt*
*buttfullalead be fair warning to where my next aim jes might be ...*

thats tillecous loufina johnson
the reverend e.m. johnson's mamma's oldest sista moved to the city
sometime ago/to seek she fortune. we calls her ole tilly fo short.
        she did acquire a fortune     just don't nobody know how
anyway
most days bout all ole tilly do is sit on her porch
till saturday night/getta shooting at them near-grown children what run
through she yard.
na/ole tilly can shoot a can off a squirrel's ass blindfold/so i know     she
don't really want to hit them half-grown fools
just lik to cuss up on the threat
hell she help raise they mammas and daddys
which is why each one speaks when they pass
        *hey aunt tilly*
        *how you today*
till saturday night they gets to shortcutn from trouble straight into ole
tilly's barrel
hollering fallnout running and carrying on
        saturday nights/most folk jes sit out     wait/for the fools to show
        up-ackout

entertain we

till bull-jean come stay wid ole tilly.
see/bull-jean's great aunty
puddn
live wid ole tilly near fifty years
till puddn pass from sugga/too high pressure and a badd cough.
    that puddn was somefine    6ft. 300lbs. of
    bitta sweet carmel/yeah!
    puddn was the onlyess one ever could handle ole tilly
anyway
they sent bull-jean to see after she aunt tilly cause word gotdown that
the ole gal had been driving    on all sides the road
na/that hefa may could shoot blindfold but she couldn't drive worth
shit
especially after the sight situation settle on she.

first two months of bull-jean's stay ole tilly
forgot bout the chil'rens/took to cussn
and shooting at bull-jean/who had hid the car keys    and the car.
well/finally ole tilly tireout got back to she usual ackn-outs.
till one saturday night
me and bull-jean was on my porch conversatn/wid cobbla and coffee
when we realize ain't been no noise long time after fools time out.
well/bull-jean lightup outta there
quick to she aunty's
found ole tilly sitting just as quiet
the kinda-grown chil'ren at her feet looking so sad

bull-jean scream
**aunt t aunt t**
**what's wrong?**
ole tilly look up say
*nuthn baby      puddn come for me/that's all*
*told me i'd better say my good-byes*
*but don't you worry none*
*i'll be back round/check on ya'll from time to time.*
at that sudda's baby's gurl start to crying
*don't leave aunty/don't you leave us na*
oh on and on.

well
it wasn't long after that.
ole tilly pass.

left the car the house and everthang of her and puddn's to bull-jean.
bull-jean drove the car back to the country/to mina
let eura's gurl's boy and him wife-just-had-chile have the house.

they name that baby loufina jr.
say ole tilly come by the baby's room wid rumbling na and
again/carrying on in the early morning.
say they run in and jr. be just laughing
and smiling lik she playing wid she
best friend-visiting
well
but/that's a whole nutha story/yeah...

## bull-jean & the question of family

*mamma mamma mamma mamma mamma mamma mamma mamma*
*mamma mamma*
*mamma mamma mamma mamma mamma mamma mamma mamma*
*mamma mamma*

shiit
i cain't hardly step off my porch widout they noise following me

*mamma mamma mamma mamma mamma mamma mamma mamma*
*mamma mamma*
*mamma mamma mamma mamma mamma mamma mamma mamma*
*maaaaaaaammma*

gotdamniit! what could they want so loud
    ohh/my nerves is badd…
my name is pontificuss devine johnson
they calls me cuss for short. i lives by mina and bull-jean and them
chil'rens what be filling they yard up. some is theys/some
is nieces nephews neighbors and cousins
shiit they all looks alik to me
noisy
mina send the chil'rens to make groceries for me friday evenings
saturday mornings i goes to mina
help supervise the chil'rens yard work.

it was a saturday morning/i was sitting

supervising

lula mae's youngest daughter child/lil bitta had just drop she son stank
by/who was distracting me from my duties cause he jes kepa sticking his
lil snot fingers in bull-jean's ears climbing crawling playing her nose/wid
him toes    till he tire out went nap under the peach tree curled up next
to mina's dog dooky who head is big as my ass    and i gots plenty ass
baby

    gotdamniit my ass is legendary in these parts!

buterra

mina sit wid me    supervise too/send bull-jean in the house wid a list
of thangs to work on. i figure i see bull-jean next saturday many to-do's
was on that sheet.

well i dose off

    let mina supervise on she own fo a time

till i feel dooky's tail beating the side of my chair/i open my eyes

and there standing this man    tall

tall/sapphire smooth/panther sleek    handsome as a newly crowned
king.

i knew i knew him/but couldn't recall where from.

thought he was utility jones boy's child they sent off for education/and
a chance

cept that boy ain't step foot-called-nor writ back home since he got him
lawyerhood.

    heard he married white

    shiit we would have welcomed her too. he just so busy trying to
    forget who

    he is he done forgot where he come from.

buterra

a closer look at the porch fella show a scar from eye to chin down the
right side his face.      muscles as big as bull-jean's/hands knicked and
callused

    make him not seem to be no desk man      though he was sharp as
    a tack.

i see/mina know him right off/she jump up and hug him tight
then hold him scar in her hand and cry      call bull-jean out.


soon as bull-jean step to the porch/eye catch that man's      her had to sit
down
her Heart stop      i know cause i felt the pause


he go to her      sit at feet say
*mamma.*
*i have missed you.*
*not a day has passed that i have not thought about you and wanted to come*
*home. after they first took me from you i cried until there weren't no tears*
*left in my twelve year old body.*
*i cried my Soul away/till my own tears flooded my Heart gonn.*
*seemed lik nobody even saw me. they just took they bible*
*used it to beat down my Heart.*

*they called you unholy*
*a sinner gonn burn in hell      said you was unnatural and unsafe for*
*children to be around/that they'd see you rot under the jail if i so much as*
*stepped to your gate.*

*afterwhile i just got mad      at you.*
*you was the strongest smartest person i knew*

*yet you didn't have the power to carry me back home.*
*i hated you for that*
*for leaving me alone*
*and scared.*
*i ran off all the time/but they always had me found.*

*soon as i got near old enough i joined the service. i wanted to fight/to die*
*really.*
*i took the most dangerous jobs/the heaviest loads the longest hours*
*saw the most shores*
*but everywhere i went everthang i did-there i was     so*
*misery went along for the ride.*
*somehow out of that small place i operated from/there must have been room*
*for light.*

*i know you was praying for me*
*i felt you      though i wouldn't let my mind tell me so.*
*you always was my Angel/my very own Saint.*
*it was you that taught me how to pray*
*how to tie my shoes/starch my pants/fish/fry chicken/fight/play ball      you*
*taught me how to cut a rose and fix it nice for the table/how to have man-*
*ners and talk to folk direct/and in the eye*
*i remember*

*you'd come home strained wid sweat/hands cut and cracking/legs dragged*
*but you always had a smile for me/always a hug and*
*as much time as i needed.*
*really in them first twelve years of my life you taught me how to be man.*

*but they took me from you*
*and they didn't know nuthn about smiling/storytelling*
*sangn me to sleep*
*or how to make a home safe for sweet dreams.*

*the man i became ain't the man you raised.*
*i have been selfish closed and driven by anger.*
*i been grievn mamma*
*all this time i been lost/unable find my way home-to feel my own Heart.*
*i didn't want to bring no children into that cruel world.*
*didn't have enough feelings*
*to keep a wo'mn     so i just kept going around the world working wid a*
*twisted mind.*

*then*
*one day i saw this little boy     he was huddled up*
*next to a dumpster near night time*
*looking dirty and shivering. he looked up*
*caught my eyes*
*and there/i saw myself     full of pain fear and hopelessness.*
*i knew wasn't nuthn i could do but pray for him/for myself*
*to find God and hold on till the way home came clear.*

*i know i always knew how to get home     guess it wasn't time befo.*

*but today God is wid me/and i am carrying my Heart on my sleeve proud*
*and sure of the man i am becoming again.*

*that boy/he didn't have no people     they was killed in a tenement fire*

*so i adopted him. we taking good care of each other.*
*he's in the yard there*
*pulling that wagon me and you made long time ago.*

*i have missed you mamma.*
*but i'm back home na*
*and ain't nobody gonn come take us apart again*
*not in this Life!*

gotdamniit
they had me crying so that day i ain't been the same since.
bull-jean
she couldn't talk for a long time/just sit hold the hands of her man-
child/crying
out the left side she face
smiling.

bull-jean's son-man say he gots two mammas na/mo Lovve-mo hugs-mo
good cooking
mo joy fo him and the boy     they got a nice lil house ova by the
mammas. son-man do building work     teach the chil'rens building on
friday nights.
     na/them sapsuckas gots another yard to run around screaming in
and gotdamniit
i think thats Blessed assurance that God is good/make everthang alright
in time
yeah!

## closing | virginia grise

*the room was full       we*
*carried disappointment heavily/though*
*loudly we laughed the world out our heads/for*
*jes a moment*

I first met bull-jean in Austin, Texas, at a small theater, sometime in the '90s. I remember it was in the middle of a relentless summer heat. I think they even boarded up the windows to keep the sun out. Maybe I'm exaggerating. I've been known to exaggerate. But I don't think the theater had air conditioning. I don't remember now. I just remember it was really, really, really hot that day.

I was with my mother. We were on our way home when she spotted a long line outside, out the door, around the corner, of people waiting to get into that theater, despite the heat. Always looking for the party, the guato, conflama, my mother asked, *What do you think is going on over there? Something is going on over there. That's where we should be. Vámonos. Let's go.* So I parked the car, and we joined the line of people waiting to be let into the theater where we would sit, packed in tight, shoulder to shoulder, sweat dripping down my thighs. It was hotter there than it was outside. I do remember that.

Not knowing what to expect, cuz back then I didn't know Sharon or bull-jean or none of dem, me and my mother sat together in that theater, in Austin, Texas. We could both feel the energy, the anticipation, the joy in that room full of people who were mostly strangers to us. Somehow, though, we ended up there, by accident or chance or divine order. I don't know but I do know it was where we were supposed to be.

That day I witnessed something I had never seen before. I've heard some people call it church but I ain't ever been to a church like that. It was rowdy and loud, raucous and ratchet and tender all at the same time. Sharon read from her performance novel and together with my mother I was introduced to the world of bull-jean and dem, just as rowdy and loud, raucous and ratchet and tender as the room. And all of it—so damn queer, and Black and Southern, in the '90s, in Texas. I don't know if it was holy or sacred but I do know it was real, that moment, that feeling, despite whatever else was happening outside in the world, inside that room, everything was, as is, should be, all right.

When it was all over, the crying, the laughing, the screaming, the applause, I waited, a bit nervous, to see what my mother would have to say about bull-jean and dem, the cussing, the fucking, all of it, but instead she just looked at me, then looked at Sharon and said, *That woman, that woman is powerful. You should meet her.* It would be a few more years before I actually met Sharon Bridgforth, before I would come to know her as a conjurer, a high priestess of the Word. But I knew then that I wanted to hold onto that moment in that theater for as long as possible. Sharon Bridgforth is powerful, is light, is magic. She is the truth. With breath and body, she creates and gives life to worlds where as a people, we can be our fullest selves, sin vergüenza, without apology or fight cuz that's the way it should be. And so it is.

Later that night, alone in my studio apartment, I sat on the floor and read *the bull-jean stories* out loud, every single word, because the Word was meant to be spoken, sung, danced, remembered, embodied, fully. Sharon, bull-jean and dem remind us that we have always been, will always be, and if we walk this world guided by Lovve we will find each other across time and space, the rowdy, the loud, the raucous, the ratchet, the tender; we will find each other in rooms of our own making; we will find each other in our shared histories and stories, spoken, sung, danced, remembered, embodied, fully.

I first met bull-jean in Austin, Texas, at a small theater, sometime in the '90s. I remember it was in the middle of a relentless summer heat.

bull-jean & dem/dey back...

     – Virginia Grise

# bull-jean/we wake

2022

*bull-jean/we wake* was written with support from Pillsbury House + Theatre, Celeste Henery, the 2020-2023 Playwrights' Center Core Writer Program, and a 2022-2023 McKnight Fellowship.

Excerpts from *bull-jean/we wake* (formerly called *bull-jean & dem/dey back*) were presented in: 2020 in the Play At Home Series; 2020 for the Austin Community College Drama Department's Radiopedemic Project; 2021 Homebound Project, performed by Stacey Karen Robinson; and Season 3 of the Who Yo People Is Podcast Series (produced by Sharon Bridgforth).

In December 2021, Pillsbury House + Theatre in Minneapolis produced a closed workshop process at the Pasadena Playhouse:

    Daniel Alexander Jones – director
    Eisa Davis – performer
    Omi Osun Joni L. Jones & Sonja Perryman – dramaturgs
    Signe Harriday – co-artistic director of Pillsbury House
    Shelby Jiggetts-Tivony & Tyrone Davis – sacred witnesses
    Nicolas Savignano – documentarian

*bull-jean/we wake* will premiere at Pillsbury House + Theatre in 2023.

## opening | celeste henery

I received my first glimpse of Sharon Bridgforth's work in the early
2000s. I was in graduate school at the University of Texas at Austin and
encountered her performance pieces through my affiliation with Black
Studies. *love conjure/blues*, *delta dandi*, and later *River See*—all staged
across campus. I hadn't seen anything like it. Each time, the theater space
filled with quick wit, resonant truths, vibrant images, and bold gestures.
People moaned, stomped, and sang. Their movements and words created a rare world that we the audience were asked to engage. I'm the type
who's more comfortable hanging on the sidelines observing, but Sharon
wants her audience to join the story and call out. Watching is only part
of the experience: in the ambit of Sharon's imagination, we also feel and
remember.

In the years since those performances, I've come to know Sharon. She has
nudged me to find my own voice and stood as an enduring figure of what
it means to live one's art. *bull-jean/we wake* is a performance novel, and
I read it at my kitchen table with my home as witness. I imagined myself
regal and affable, like Sharon, in order to travel into this hybrid work,
shift into her language, and settle into the intimate spaces where her people reside. I also invoked something higher, as her creations tend to ferry
you to uncommon places. I landed in bull-jean's village, a place of kin and
community where new and old characters weave a story across time and
lives. The pages crackled with Sharon's usual humor and some intrigue,
but most of all I felt the breadth of her wisdom and heart.

*bull-jean/we wake* is a tale of healing. The narrator gregariously draws us
into their world by relaying the interactions and struggles of their community all the while telling of their own. We take in the heartfelt strife
of people wishing to be more comfortable in themselves, even as their
sense of who they are ages and alters. We discover how grace arrives to
support their transformation. bull-jean affirms my sense that healing may
be the consequence of timing as much as a willingness to grow. Sharon

makes the invisible visible, by showing greater processes and forces at play. No hurt, doubt, or hope goes without notice or guidance. My own recognition of spirit is restored and renewed by its unabashed presence in Sharon's art.

We also rendezvous with the ancestors. Through her work, Sharon displays how our predecessors live around and in us, sometimes stepping forward as allies. bull-jean conjures the legacy of Sharon's and so many other Black families' migrations from the U.S. South westward, and her own movements back and forth. It reads like an ethnography of ancestral memory documenting the intertwined experiences of exile and the perseverance foundational to this ambulatory history. As a student of Black life whose Blackness originates in South America, I'm grateful to be invited into this vibrant American space, to take a seat under a shaded tree, and to learn about the aches and affections of this community. It's a wonder to see Black memory and alterity exist comfortably, and richly. When old caney sharp bangs his cane, I feel a long line of Sharon's kin finding their words, encountering their troubles, and having their labors honored. I also discern the whispers of my own ancestral inheritance and wonder about its influence in my creative endeavors and healing.

Through years of experiencing Sharon's work, I've come to understand it as a summons into sacred time, where the questions of our spirit can be heard and where we might receive answers. "See me" inaugurates *bull-jean/we wake*—and what follows are incantations and memories that set the story and narrator in motion. Sharon doesn't craft god-like figures, but a community of characters with flaws as well as the capaciousness to transform and help others. bull-jean herself is one of these folks, and so is dat black mermaid man lady. Moving in sacred time, both reappear from earlier pieces reminding us of the living tradition out of which Sharon creates. This tradition appeals to us to carry forth with our burdens, to embrace wherever we are and where we might go. Who else but a Black mermaid with fishes and pearls traveling the sky could animate our capacity to breathe anywhere?

I locate Sharon's work in a larger network of international women writers exploring questions of belonging and experimenting with genre. Shailja Patel's *Migritude* and Werewere Liking's *It Shall be of Jasper and Coral (A Song-Novel)* use hybrid designs to tell complex gendered stories about the physical and emotional displacements of colonialism. Each of these writers transmits pain and hope through the power of their observant eye and the beauty of their language. Each uses their distinct diasporic vernacular to help remember and envision this bittersweet world anew.

The timing of *bull-jean/we wake* feels important. It arrives several years into the isolation of the pandemic, as things open back up and we confront the insecurities of a planet and a humanity in obvious distress. bull-jean offers a poetics for this juncture. No matter the difficulty, we can find healing and creativity. We can turn to those who came before us to show us the way through catastrophe, as they have done before. We can be buoyed by their memory. Like the jazz aesthetic Sharon works in, we can skillfully improvise, listening for what longs to emerge.

I also recognize Sharon's work as an artistic referent by which to navigate these bewildering times. Her art invokes in my mind's eye the Southern Cross, the constellation of bright stars most visible in the southern hemisphere. Their lights steer a metaphoric turn south, towards the spaces of our origins, and the crossroads where our imaginations intersect with the cosmos. With Sharon's work as guide, we are encouraged to re-orient, to become students of our soul's birthright, and to use it generatively in our "craftspersonship," as I've heard her name it. In her work, I find I am welcomed and inspired, and if I were in need, bull-jean herself would take me under her care. And just maybe, I'd see dat Black mermaid and be reminded of all that's possible, or all that might be possible, if, like Sharon, we ask it to take shape.

– Celeste Henery, April 2022

*See me.*

*Head thrown back*
*shoulders shaking*
*hips swaying*
*laughing*
*twirling time.*

*See me.*
*Notice how Light*
*breaks through*
*the fractures.*
*See me*

*raw and undone.*
*Brittle and broken.*
*Unable to soften.*
*Hard to hold.*
*So imperfect.*
*And Brilliant.*
*And Free.*

*I want you to See me.*

*And know that though*
*I was never able to piece myself together*
*I was whole.*
*And so are you.*

*Unroot the stuck*
*walk through it.*
*Let it churn and crumble away.*
*Remember that I showed you what to do*

*drop into your shimmer*
*and Shine*
*throw your head back*
*shake your ass*
*and dance damnit.*

*Call my name*
*and See me.*
*Open your arms*
*and receive*
*all*
*my*
*Love*

**1.**

*stacks*
*big bill*
*bull-jean*
*snacks*
*great big mamma*
*one of the ones we ain't never seent*
*doctor black*
*who dat*
*shiny*
*da family*
*ole caney sharp*
*crunch*
*shiny mamma*
*mr fine*
*mr sweeter*
*bubba irish*
*mr strut*
*mr strut mamma*
*mina*
*bull-jean son-man boy-child jr*
*the young peoples*
*the children mina done passed she fan making onto*
*angels with fins and black black skin*
*dat black mermaid man lady with fishes and fishes and pearls flowing*
*all the way down past behind*

*ga ga ga   ga ga ga   ga ga ga*
*hush*
*great big mamma from long line of wo'mns and them*
*great big mamma the ones we ain't never seen*
*us*
*folk from porch and yard*
*stacks dog queen*
*bull-jean mamma*
*bull-jean son-man*
*lil bits*

## 1.

clap clap   clap
     clap clap
clap clap   clap
     clap clap
clap clap   clap
     clap clap
clap clap   clap
     clap clap
clap clap   clap
     clap clap

**9.**

stacks
*stacks*

big bill
*big bill*

bull-jean
*bull-jean*

snacks
*snacks*

great big mamma
*great big mamma*

one of the ones we ain't never seent
*one of the ones we ain't never seent*

doctor black
*doctor black*

who dat
*who dat*

shiny
*shiny*

da family
*da family*

ole caney sharp
*ole caney sharp*

crunch
*crunch*

shiny mamma
*shiny mamma*

mr fine
*mr fine*

mr sweeter
*mr sweeter*

bubba irish
*bubba irish*

mr strut
mr strut

mr strut mamma
mr strut mamma

mina
mina

bull-jean son-man boy-child jr
bull-jean son-man boy-child jr

the young peoples
the young peoples

the children mina done passed she fan making onto
the children mina done passed she fan making onto

angels with fins and black black skin
angels with fins and black black skin

dat black mermaid man lady with fishes and fishes and pearls flowing
dat black mermaid man lady with fishes and fishes and pearls flowing

all the way down past behind
all the way down past behind

ga ga ga    ga ga ga    ga ga ga
ga ga ga    ga ga ga    ga ga ga

hush
hush

great big mamma from long line of wo'mns and them
great big mamma from long line of wo'mns and them

great big mamma the ones we ain't never seen
great big mamma the ones we ain't never seen

us
us

folk from porch and yard
folk from porch and yard

stacks dog queen
stacks dog queen

bull-jean mamma
bull-jean mamma

*bull-jean son-man*
*bull-jean son-man*

*lil bits*
*lil bits*

## 7.

*stacks*
*stacks*

*big bill*
*big bill*

*bull-jean*
*bull-jean*

*snacks*
*snacks*

*great big mamma*
*great big mamma*

*one of the ones we ain't never seent*
*one of the ones we ain't never seent*

*doctor black*
*doctor black*

*who dat*
*who dat*

*shiny*
*shiny*

*da family*
*da family*

*ole caney sharp*
*ole caney sharp*

crunch
crunch

shiny mamma
shiny mamma

mr fine
mr fine

mr sweeter
mr sweeter

bubba irish
bubba irish

mr strut
mr strut

mr strut mamma
mr strut mamma

mina
mina

bull-jean son-man boy-child jr
bull-jean son-man boy-child jr

the young peoples
the young peoples

the children mina done passed she fan making onto
the children mina done passed she fan making onto

angels with fins and black black skin
angels with fins and black black skin

dat black mermaid man lady with fishes and fishes and pearls flowing
dat black mermaid man lady with fishes and fishes and pearls flowing

all the way down past behind
all the way down past behind

ga ga ga     ga ga ga     ga ga ga
ga ga ga     ga ga ga     ga ga ga

hush
hush

99

*great big mamma from long line of wo'mns and them*

*great big mamma the ones we ain't never seen*

*us*

*folk from porch and yard*

*stacks dog queen*

*bull-jean mamma*

*bull-jean son-man*

*lil bits*

**8.**

stacks lay she voice out all up and around juicy lucy's
big bill stroke the piano.
bull-jean blow the jug.
together they move in slight sways
with sounds that bust open the heart.
ever so slow
they step
sway step
sway

yessuh
them
they keep everbody
tilted and on edge.

them
they rock
we roll.
they
they tilt
we quiver.
us
we raise
they swagger

all step sway step.

together we make black heat.
smoke the entire joint
till it crack like thunder.
yessuh
we bring our own selves to a hallelujah crumble
and wail.

but what i want to talk about today is

they old.

that's right.
folk rather fight than hear it said
but truth is

bull-jean
big bill
stacks
them
they
old.

oh yeah
they looks tasty
can still stew the room.
but
i hear they bones creeking
i feel they knees wobbling
i see the slow of they

and i remember when.

and too
i know that snacks been sent here cause
great big mamma want her to keepa check on
they
and them ole asses.
see

what had happened was
snacks
who real name is perceva louise baddabreaux.
she a ity bitty thing
look good cnough to eat
so we calls her
snacks.
anyways
snacks is a child of one of the ones we ain't never seent.
one a them from great big mamma from a long line of.
snacks carry they strong.
it is said that
she have stopped many a real big mens with ill intentions storming
towards she
with a planted stance and stare
and that she done prayed many a fool back from stupid.
ummhumm
anyways

snacks gots some lots of great big mamma in her.
it were snacks that made stacks go to doctor black
well
she made stacks go to great big mamma
who made stacks go to doctor black
anyways

on this day
them they rocking
we rolling.
they they tilting
we quivering
but before we could rise

up from yonder come a vision

who know were it
a mans a womans neither both or other
but what we did know is
they was sho nuff fine.
they stroll on in
quiet the room
with all they glory.
come up from back singing

all pause in wonder

who dat

**9.**

and jus lik that
the weather changed.
all the sunny that was
melted into darkness
and the darkness parted
and it rained
and it rained
and it rained

and since shiny didn't lik getting wet
shiny ran and whined and whimpered all down the way.
she got so caught up in her fruslustrations
that she could not see the beauty in what was unfolding round her
as the clouds poured themselves on her head and round her feet.
shiny jus ran
and shiny whined
and shiny whimpered
and she shivered

**3.**

*What can I do to bring sweetness to you today?*

*I think I should ask one of the children*
*one of the really young ones.*

*They know everything.*

**4.**

                                          *stacks*

i told that mafuka                  *big bill*

i said                  *bull-jean*

looka here                                  *snacks*

i said            *great big mamma*

hummph                  *one of the ones we ain't never seent*

i said                      *doctor black*

i told that mafuka        *who dat*

i said    *shiny*

when have you ever         *da family*

i said                 *ole caney sharp*

fool what                 *crunch*

i said            *shiny mamma*

hecksnaw              *mr fine*

i told that mafuka    *mr sweeter*

i said         *bubba irish*

looka here                          *mr strut*

i said    *mr strut mamma*

i remember when           *mina*

i said          *bull-jean son-man boy-child jr*          *the young peoples*

mafuka                          *the children mina done passed she*

hush.


## 8.


we calls her stacks
cause look like she made of boulders
packed and stacked just right.
yessuh
the only soft spot on her is she eyes.
which her heart speak brightly through.

stacks is sweet as can be
real good to look at
and always dressed to the nines
even on her do nothing days.
see
stacks make she own clothes.
had to
cause wasn't no way
she could find something to fit all them boulders she gots
and too
stacks say clothes have always betrayed her.
the wy'mn's clothes weren't never gone be right
and the men's clothes looked good off

but they was always a square away from right on.
so stacks took to sewing what she inside self knew her outside to be.
stacks say she come to like the sound of the sewing machine
say the feel of cloth running through her fingers
help her breathe.
most days
stacks sit down at dusk
and sew and sew and she sew
except friday night thru midday sunday
which is her
bull-jean
big bill
and da family
singing time at juicy lucy's.
ummhumm
see

what had happened was
bull-jean is stacks mamma third husband sister chile
big bill is stacks second cousin on she daddy side
and da family
well that's a whole nutha story yeah.
anyways

stacks
bull-jean
big bill
and da family

sing friday night thru midday sunday.

stacks make all they clothes.
hecks stacks made clothes for all the ones from counties around
that couldn't never fully find a way for they outsides to match they
insides.
anyways
them three come rolling by to meet da family
make way to juicy lucy's all packed tight slow walking and pressed
hummmhumm
   just looking at all that meat make you need to eat
    make you gotta just put something in your mouth when they walk by.
which is how my hoe cake stand got to be placed in front of stacks house
friday night thru midday sunday
cause the sight of them make everbody
need to taste da hottness.
i figured
i could look eat and count my change.
yessuh
i serves the peoples an excuse to come close to stacks steps
fill they mouth
and savor all that black heat pouring out.
anyways

friday night thru midday sunday
big bill on piano
bull-jean direct da family
and stacks lead the song.

together they move in slight gestures
tiny tilts
and ever so slow steps
keep everbody on edge
and perched to pop.
yessuh

time they done
everthing
all thru the streets
and all up in juicy lucy's
done been simmered
by heat of they release


## 4.


ole caney sharp
is bull-jean's great uncle on she daddy side.
ole caney sharp used to live way back over there
but some how he manage to bang he cane long the road
till he show up here
out from the woods to the other side just before the swamp
he land at that house next to crunch.

they say ole caney sharp can fly

## 10.

and see

shiny mamma so gotdaggnit good looking
that just feeling her close by
done made many a good fool do bad things.
all with good sense know
don't look too hard or too long
else you find yourself
in a situation
chasing after her impossible to please behind that ain't gone never
chase you back.
anyways
some just calls her a good business wo'mn.
   i calls her mean and selfish and rude and
   like that time i had chasedt her and she didn't never even look me in
   the eye
   just had me growing her groceries in my yard and then
   and then
   and
thankfully
for me
they sent me to great big mamma
who stared me in my loosed eyes till
they straighten back in my head.
and
and

and
whatever crazy got loosed in my mind was
too scared of great big mamma to hang around
and so

anyways.

it were widely known and reported
that though didn't nobody know who shiny daddy were
everbody knew shiny mamma
had three boyfriends all shiny growing up life.

one of shiny mamma's boyfriends was just as fine as shiny mamma were.
she kept a place on her arm for him.
he owned his own very large very nice house a couple of towns over.
they say that way back when the whites on he daddy's side died off
they had provisioned the Coloured side into what was left.
which the Coloured then used every bit of smarts
labor and conjurations to hold on to protect and build from
despite all the whitelash that came upon them.
yessuh
it is said that for all time anytime white folk think of torching taking or
hanging
any of mr fine's family
they muscles cave inwards and crush they bones till all that's left
is they hate filled thoughts
which stay trapped in they minds.
anyways

whenever shiny ended up at she aunty and uncle's for too long
we know
shiny mamma were laid up over to mr fine's house.
ummhummm.
well like i say
she gots everybody minds turned all back in we heads
so we like that she return from mr fine's giggling
and stepping light.

one boyfriend
mr sweeter
used to make shiny mamma groceries.
i tried to tell him
don't do it mann
but he no hear me.
po thing.
anyways

he have a farm two towns in the other direction of mr fine.
mr sweeter come from a line of sharecroppers that eventually
bought they land clear and using they white friend
bubba irish as cover to purchase they sharecropped lands
and all the lands on all sides that land.
bubba irish and he family live on one of the sides
pretend it all his
but we all know
and the paperwork know the truth.
anyways

mr sweeter the biggest man we ever seent.

he connection with the land

seemed to grow him tall tall and mountain wide.

seem like

all he time in open air and dirt and feeling free

fill he soul with honey.

every week

mr sweeter roll up on he horse

leave satchels of fruits and vegetables and meats

fresh off his farm on the porch for shiny to take prepare and share with

we

while he reach down and pull shiny mamma up onto he horse

ride away.

days after shiny get the meat cooked and the groceries put up

shiny mamma back

looking drifty and starry eyed.


that last one were shiny mamma favorite of all.

mr strut.

he real smart.

he the only one allowed to come in the house.

shiny mamma say

a hard dick don't have no conscious—so wasn't go be no laying around

or staying over.

that were her way of protecting shiny

from some of the evil things that had happened to her as a child.

anyways

mr strut live in a little shack behind his mamma house down the way.
he mamma don't think no wo'mn good enough for her boy
and he don't love no wo'mn more than he mamma
so wasn't no way mr strut was ever
gonn be more than a pass by kind of man.
so
mr strut come on saturdays.
he always come with a new book for shiny
thinking of where or how he got them books
were too terrifying to speculate on
cause in them days white peoples
guarded they books with nooses.
anyways

mr strut taught shiny how to read.
how to dream really.
they'd sit out on the porch saturday mornings
discussing last week's book
and eating whatever meats was leftover from mr sweeter's last batch
till time for mr strut and shiny mamma to get on over to juicy lucy's to
ready for
bull-jean
big bill
stacks
and da family.

look like some of them each
mr fine mr sweeter mr strut and shiny mamma

made the all of shiny.

filled with dreaming and left alone
shiny became a sensitive child.
able hear through silence
and with all she skin
unblocked
shiny spoke to the night
and the stars responded
with cycloning stillness
shiny grew into sheself
whole fine and free.
rugged sweet strutting smart
and a good business person.
yessuh
our shiny be quite special.


## 10.

bull-jean had put that lil ole shack back she and mina house
to a beautiful order.
after the visit with doctor black snacks brought stacks right on over to it.
na what i want to know is
how did bull-jean get word to put that lil ole shack in order.
and how did snacks know that bull-jean had received the word.
and why stacks let they take charge.

anyways

snacks done made she mind up that stacks
is her very own number one project.
you can hear them fussing from way yonda.
cause stacks trying to refuse she medicine
lawd2day

we all be glad when stacks done mending.
we tired of they combustioning and carrying on.
plus

we scared.

can't bare the sight of stacks suffering.
or the thought of loosing she.

anyways.

some mornings
before they get rolling
we all bunch up on the porch
of stacks lil ole shack back of bull-jean and mina house.
we sit quiet.
listen to the birds.
have our coffee.
rest together in the rising sun.

this one morning

stacks shuffle out on the porch
ease down to sit while snacks fetch she morning potion.
all breathe in silence
till stacks say
i have always hated these things.
stacks grab she titties
i have wanted them gone since the day they showed theyselves.
all big and uninvited.
they robbed me of who i felt myself to be.
got in the way of everything.
made it hard to look in the mirror and see myself.
took away my desire to let a wo'mn take me in fully.
kept a wall of voices going off in my head all the time.
look like right when i donn sewed my way into myself
suiting the curve of them into a rightful expression
where i could finally step and stretch out with them
fully myself

here this come.

i wonder
if all them years of festering with hate for these here things
turned in on me.
became the poison that is now eating me alive.
these things
these breasteses
will be gone soon.

i hope i survive the cut.

## 16.

*How can I show up for you more.*
*How can I make you feel safe.*
*How can I tell you that we made it.*
*How can I express how perfect you are just as you are.*
*How can I reveal your strength to you.*
*How can I thank you.*
*How many ways can I say*
*I Love you.*

## 11.

bull-jean out there dragging fell wood
to chop and place in everybody home.
that real nice
cept
it summer
and it so gotdamnits hot
just looking at them pieces of wood she dragging over
make everybody heart race.

we beg mina
please help.
but
we all understand
well we all understand
cept bull-jean      who slow on the up take of she insides
we all understand
bull-jean scared her
long long best friend stacks
gone go to da LAWD before time
before she

but gotdamnits
we all feel like da LAWD coming early
for us
with all the heat and worry
bull-jean carrying round.
anyways

one morning we see mina
send bull-jean son-man boy-child jr over
    bull-jean's son-man boy jr is named after mina
anyways

on this day bull-jean son-man boy-child jr
perch up on bull-jean and mina porch
cooling heself with he fan and eyelashes
that seem to reach and curl the sun

back into the light of his light light eyes
he long long black hair
pull tightly into the black black of he skin
which paint a powerful picture
of all them that was
and all coming
who seem to always
be swimming round he head
looking at us through he eyes
anyways

what had happened was
we thanking da LAWD
cause we know
bull-jean love
bull-jean son-man boy-child jr
more than she own self.
so bull-jean son-man boy-child jr
just showing up to perch
were the best possible way for bull-jean
deep down to connect with she way up.

we watch
quiet
wait
still.
try not to distract from the situation.

then
bull-jean come round from back a woods dragging what fell
and saw bull-jean son-man boy-child jr

bull-jean stop

just stand there looking into
she bull-jean son-man boy-child jr eyes
they staring
so still and so powerfully long
they knock stacks dog queen into a standing up sleep
maybe us too.
anyways

eventually
who know how long
bull-jean let everything she had dragged
fall round she.
she step front of it
nodd to bull-jean son-man boy-child jr/say it hot.
bull-jean son-man boy-child jr bat he eyes
get up
grab he bull-jean hand
and off they go on in the house
to mina and bull-jean son-man
who waiting
OHHHH thankyee LAWD we think.
don't nobody say nothing out loud

so as not to distrub the possible opening
the moment were holding.

we just nodd and rock
and cry a little.

## 11. 3.

every time shiny come by
ole caney sharp get to banging he cane on the porch
rocking and crying
talking bout
they here
they here
thank da LAWD they here.

he call shiny over
snatch shiny in for deep eyeball stares
till look like shiny get dizzy.
then ole caney sharp push shiny on with he cane
and get to singing
songs from before before
in ole folk language that we can't hardly understand

but do.

## 5. 5. 5. 5. 5.

mina had taught the young peoples
how to weave.
make fans.

fans so colorful
the swirl of they
move all sight and sound.

each wave tickle the air.
take you way past
what known.

like on this day

when it came clear
that mina need a healing.

bull-jean son-man boy-child jr
lead all the children mina done passed she fan making on to
pour into mina and bull-jean yard and porch
running and laughing and skipping and fanning and tumbling
they wave the air

till mina come out
sit on porch.

then all the children mina done passed she fan making on to

circle mina and bull-jean house tight tighter
with fans flicking they
wave the air
circle right
drop left
running and laughing and skipping and fanning and tumbling they
flick wave circle drop
clap
flick wave circle drop clap
they twirl
flick wave circle drop clap twirl
they play
flick wave circle drop clap twirl play
they call the moon
pray to earth
running and laughing and skipping and fanning and tumbling they
flick wave circle drop clap twirl play call pray

till the trees tilt

and out fly angels with fins and black black skin
and long long braids curling round pouring out all over
up and down the road and back singing
and dat black mermaid man lady with fishes and fishes and pearls flowing all the way down past behind brush through clouds come down
ga ga ga      ga ga ga      ga ga ga
and all the children mina done passed she fan making on to
running and laughing and skipping and fanning and tumbling

flick wave circle drop clap twirl play call pray
flick wave circle drop clap twirl play call pray
on and on and on
closer and closer to mina
angels with fins and black black skin
and long long braids curling round singing
dat black mermaid man lady with fishes and fishes and pearls flowing
all the way down past behind
ga ga ga   ga ga ga   ga ga ga
all the children mina done passed she fan making on to
they disappear into mina.

fans fall all around she.
and all there is

Is.

bull-jean son-man boy-child jr
on porch next to mina
he look up
he breathe
he smile

he grab mina hand
take she back on in the house.

only we there now
eyes filled with clouds swimming fans
and wonder

till suddenly


## 7.

*angels with fins and black black skin*
sabsucka *dat black mermaid man lady with fishes and fishes and pearls*
swishswasha
*flowing all the way down past behind*
twiststa *ga ga ga  ga ga ga  ga ga ga*
liar
*hush*
bastard *great big mamma from long line of wo'mns and them*
fool *great big mamma the ones we ain't never seen*
back de fuk up
*us*
git all the fuk way from here *folk from porch and yard*
run i say
*stacks dog queen*
run
mafuka.

shit.


## 16.

bull-jean say more in she mind than she do out loud.
she think she be talking but really she only be thinking.
that was what got in the way of she and mina

all that damn thinking no talking.
even though mina could read bull-jean mind
she say she shouldn't have to.
we agree.

bull-jean
we yelling
try to pull words out your head more than only sometimes.
well
anyways.

but when bull-jean do speak
her words so beautiful
make your heart hurt from opening.
but that don't mean shit if that beauty don't hit the air.

that is why crunch yelling
talk gurl talk
course all bull-jean do then is chuckle on down the way.

till na.
bull-jean done took to sitting with hush
who be over there
hurling them cussalating out and around.
when hush cussalating
we know everything alright
it's hush quiet that worrisome.

see

shifts from on high
move through hush
before they land on us.

seeing bull-jean there
sitting looking all grumbled next to hush
very worrisome

this trouble hush to quiet

damnits we say

## 13.

*I see now that I haven't allowed my heart to melt in quite awhile.*

*What is the price of that*
*I wonder*

## 17.

we don't stare too long or look too hard at snacks.
fools that do that can't seem to get they eyes unhooked
be swirling in moon light looking for the sun.
anyways

snacks show up when a healing is needed.
usually
we know snacks coming
cause we hear hush quiet.

snacks come carrying all that was
and all that coming in the touch of she hands.
snacks lay hands
latch eyes
get to whispering and rocking and moaning
till she whirl lift dirt and wind.
when she done
it did.
grace be there carrying in the new.
but every now and then
grace don't come.
every now and then
snacks gots to bring great big mamma long line of wo'mns and them.

that what happen with stacks.
grace wasn't enough to clear what was holding stacks.
that's why snacks call all in.

bull-jean big bill and da family great big mamma great big mamma the
ones we ain't never seen great big mamma from long line of wo'mns and
them bull-jean son-man bull-jean son-man boy-child jr doctor black
snacks shiny shiny mamma mr fine mr sweeter mr strut ole caney sharp
crunch lil bits stacks dog queen

us

all there
rumbling the road.

that's how grace came down for stacks.


## 23.

see

what had happened was
that who dat singer name be grace.
grace feel the call from way wherever grace had been.
we thinking wherever grace had been
stacks had been a plenty too.
anyways
see what had happened was
stacks never did like too many heads up in she kitchen.
she say that's how mess that can't get cleaned get made.
so stacks always have done most of she cooking on she own.
my guess is bull-jean big bill and da family
already knowd that who dat singer name be grace
and you know great big mamma the ones we ain't never seen
great big mamma from long line of wo'mns
always know everything

and for sho stacks dog queen know'd
but us
we didn't know shit

anyways

what I'm saying is
stacks like to keep some business to she self.
so though we was floored

we wasn't surprised by grace.


**9. 9.**

*We are drowning*
*in the past*

*sometimes*


**21.**

*us*

i is too tired          *folk from porch and yard*
to cuss you right na.                    *stacks dog queen*
so go on                    *bull-jean mamma*

git the fuk away from here        *bull-jean son-man*
mafuka

                                                    *lil bits*


## 33.


they come in threes them
dustn up the street
they stomping the road
ga ga ga     ga ga ga     ga ga ga
they swirl the air
ga ga ga     ga ga ga     ga ga ga
they break iron tracks cross make ditches open dirt
new paths on the road
ga ga ga     ga ga ga     ga ga ga
they spew rocks
they hurry dust
they whirl toss
they
ga ga ga     ga ga ga     ga ga ga

when they finally arrive
all falls and settles
till all what left is
they
in stillness

and they is
the most teeninchy bits of fury and fuss you ever done seent
ga ga ga      ga ga ga      ga ga ga
stand there
stare everbody shut up

till finally
after
ga ga ga      ga ga ga      ga ga ga
shock and pause
and shut us dafuk up
finally

they dust and whirl and stomp
back on down to where ever the hecks
they come from


## 21.

stacks situation call for long walk.

bull-jean big bill and da family
hummm moan walk
silent
silent
hummm moan walk

silent

along the way
some shout from porch and yard
some join and walk
silent
silent
hummm moan walk

lil bits burst through with
notes from high
and ole caney sharp and crunch get to tap tapping they canes
as lil bits pour out the sound of Love round us.

all look up look around look down look ahead
receive what there.
see

and what had happened was
the Light opened the sky and the road rose
and there we see
great big mamma and bull-jean son-man boy-child jr
shoot up up up
towards great big mamma the ones we ain't never seen
great big mamma from long line of wo'mns
who hand them something
we don't know what
and blink them back down to us.

and we Know
more

sooncome


**27.**

*I can't do this*
*I can't feel all these feelings*
*I refuse to fall all the way out*

*so I stiffen back my tears*
*and will the depth of my feelings be quiet.*

*I am afraid*

**6.**

all still in the hard of what stacks had said
bout she breastesess.

cept crunch who shout
who cut cutting?
what cut cutting?
i declare that sabsucka cut

best not show they self round here.
where cut at gotdamnits?

yeah
crunch can't hear like she used to could.
she always be close to the point
a little to the side of it
just enough to tickle a room.
yessuh

crunch cussing and banging she cane on the porch
got stacks to giggling
which got us to giggling
which didn't stop crunch at all
she just keep a banging that cane and yelling threats at cut.
till stacks take she last sip of coffee
shuffle back into she lil ole shack in back house bull-jean
chuckling.
and full of light.


**31.**

*I will learn to soften the hard of the*
*rocked over stagnant stench of my heart.*

*I will learn to laugh instead of snapping*

to stretch and turn and shift

instead of roaring as I run away.
I will learn to cry.

To rest before rising.
I will learn to hear the birds singing

in the stench of a new dawning.
I will learn to be still

to presence myself and breathe.
I will learn to offer what I hope to receive.

I will learn over and over and over again
and over and over and over again

to See the Light

maybe


## 24.

one day
we counsel
cause we see mina shifting and stacks struggling
done got bull-jean so deep in she self
look like she lost.

so we sent big bill
go sit on bull-jean porch
hopefully pull bull-jean out.

ventually
bull-jean come out on she porch
take a seat
say
i feel like a hot kettle too empty to whistle.
i got no steam left.
i done capped over what wants to rise for so long
everything donn seeped out the sides.
till now i feel like a broken vessel

i gots no pretty words to put on this.
nothing to drape this ugly with.
i am exhausted
in my soul
i am tired

and i am afraid.

i been churning my afraid for so long
it's done risen the rage buried underneath it to the surface.
i am scared of what might happen if my rage gets out.
so i been trying to clamp it in
this afraid of love leaving
this knowing that love leaves

this rage at love leaving
i donn clamped this down
since my mamma and my daddy
who i loved so much but all my love couldn't save
and they got taken from me
right in front of me
and i just thought
deep down
i just thought that if i loved hard enough
somehow
i would see them again

but no

and now too
here i is again
with death walking so close to my deep long loves
right in front of me
look like Love is leaving.
thats seem to be all i see right now
when i look at them
all i see is they leaving.
my heart
it has crumbled into my churning
till i think it's gonn

my heart.
Love has been my how

my why and my all
and if Love keeps leaving
i got no reason for my heart anyways.
so look like it can just stay gone.

i gots no prayers left in me. *i gots no prayers left in me.*
so i'm bout to let go of all the nice i used to had decided to be *decided to be*
i ain't showing up do a gotdanmits thang for nobody. *thang for nobody.*
no singing *no singing*
no moving da line *no moving da line*
no sitting *no sitting*
no listening *no listening*
no lessons *no lessons*
nuthn *nuthn*
everybody *everybody*
can kiss my Coloured behind *can kiss my Coloured behind*
and leave me dafuk alone. *and leave me dafuk alone.*
i *i*
is *is*
done. *done.*

look like time stop
everything freeze
the wind pause
even hush quiet.

big bill she shiver

oh oh
i say


**27.**

big bill bull-jean

shiny     big mamma  *I'm afraid I have no words*

mr fine   ole caney sharp *nothing to say*

*no well to dive into.*

mr strut mamma     the young people gina

dat black mermaid man lady with fishes and fishes *Nothing is all there is*


**40.**

on this day
crunch make shiny take her to find that
sabsucking cut cutting mafucka.
leave us all to sit in the smiling air
with our heartache
bout stacks situation.

that is till great big mamma come busting up the road
which scare the bajeebas out us.
usually we got to go to great big mamma
or great big mamma send snacks to come get us

but can't nobody recall ever
seeing great big mamma busting the road up.
you could hear everybody heart beating louder and faster
closer she got
the more our breaths got caught in our throats
had us sounding like a pack of creek frogs choking in the night
anyways

great big mamma stomp right on up
the porch of stacks lil ole shack back of bull-jean and mina house
she get on up there and say
it come to me in a dream.


## 5.


mina don't speak english no more
but we understand everything she say.
look like mina done took to dreaming she way back in time.
time when she was an island girl full of yucca and platanos.
with a mango heart
mina she tell me again and again
the story of she mamma and daddy long gone
like how they came by boat and back of truck
looking to make they new mark and better life
only to find white mens with murderous eyes
swarming they not grown daughter body.

mina say she mamma and daddy move they in the break of light
run up to a moving train
they lift she on
but they where not able to climb up
before the swarm of murderous eyed white mens
snatch they back with pounding words and sticks and fists.

trying to will that image from she eyes
mina say she went blind for years after that
say she don't remember nothing for a time after
don't know how she got here
don't know how she survived or what happened
cept somehow in her blanketed state
she seen dat black mermaid man lady swimming
with fishes and fishes and pearls flowing all the way down past behind
call her here and there till she wake up yonder.

mina say
dat black mermaid man lady
with fishes and fishes and pearls flowing all the way down past behind

here na

## 7. 7. 7. 7. 7. 7. 7.

*running and laughing and skipping and fanning and tumbling*
*running and laughing and skipping and fanning and tumbling*

*running and laughing and skipping and fanning and tumbling they circle*
*running and laughing and skipping and fanning and tumbling*
*tapping they tapping they tapping faster*
*they running and laughing and skipping and fanning and tumbling they*
*circle till bees and butterflies and birds join up*
*and the trees lean and*

*ga ga ga   ga ga ga   ga ga ga*
*ga  ga ga ga  ga ga ga  ga ga ga*

*thunder and the sky open*
*and out fly angels with fins and black black skin*
*and long long braids curling round pouring out all over*
*up and down the road and back singing*
*and dat black mermaid man lady with fishes and fishes and pearls flowing*
*all the way down past behind brush through clouds come down*
*and*

## 4.

then i got snatched into da council meeting
bull-jean donn loss she mind they say
cussn like hush and pushing peoples away
sitting on she ass all day in de house
looking mean and
acting a fool

you need to git ova there n help she.

why me i wonder
but don't say.
next thing i know i'm out front da road
walking toward bull-jean's gate.
how they do that i mumble i sick of they always snatching and shoving
and telling people what to do i ain't got to do nuthn they say i say
as i open bull-jean gate
i see she door open
damnits i say
here i is once again
in the middle of they will.
but i go on in
where bull-jean rise when she see me
like she been waiting
she let me take she hand
and walk she out through yard and gate
pass ole caney sharp and crunch porch
over by hush house
down through the brush
cross da swamp
through the backawoods
yonder.

you will know what to do once you get there they had said
hummp
how i gonn know and what i gonn do if we get wherever there is and if
i know what to do why they gots to always be telling me what to do. i

gonn do what the hecks i feel like doing
and i just might not do a thang damnits i mumbles
my mumbles make bull-jean chuckle
walk a little lighter
and faster
and faster
till i find that i have to stop me mumbles
and breathe

then suddenly i see
my breathing
and bull-jean faster faster
taking us exactly
where we need to go.
as we cross yonder
bull-jean say
i see blood everywhere
and bodies that float and fly.
i see lashed backs bent in the sun
and hands too thick from scars to close.
always always always there be wailing
and bodies hanging from trees.

and then there is my mamma and my daddy.
smiling and waving good bye
before i arrive.

i used to try to drink it all away

but i got fed up of my own fool self from drinking
and too apparently drinking didn't help
cause all these years later
after drinking
after stopping drinking
after juggling wy'mns hoping they'd quiet the blood
after finding my one wo'mn
my very own one
here it is
all back again
flooding me with its stench.

what here i ask.

bull-jean look at me long time.
finally she say
mad.
mad donn come back.
this time i think
it just might kill me.

oh oh
i think
as me and bull-jean fall out yonder
breathing loud and fast fast
under thick clouds and shifting sky

**2.**

all falled out i see the blood too
and in the pouring blood
i see bull-jean and all the kind all the help
all the teaching she donn donn
all the food and hugs and home and songs and listening she donn gave
all the showing up and staying all the returning and pushing forward
all the hearts she donn touched and opened and soothed
i see all the people all the people she donn held Light open for and
i remember
i mad too
from walking with a torn apart heart
i remember
walking in the blood shattered and sent
i remember
the lashed backs bent in the sun
and hands too thick from scars to close.
i remember
the wailing
and bodies hanging from trees.
i remember
mamma and daddy
smiling and waving good bye
before i arrive.
i remember

till the sky break

and the earth fill up angels with fins and black black skin
and long long braids curling round singing and
dat black mermaid man lady with fishes and fishes and pearls flowing
all the way down past behind
come up through the dirt
and pour itself down into me
and we rise we
grab bull-jean hand
and take her

fly


## 31.

till suddenly

we back laid out on the grass
front bull-jean and mina yard

we look up
tears rolling down
the right side we face.
we there
who know how long

till ole caney sharp and crunch get to shouting from they porches
breathe fools

breathe.

the startle of they

jump start me and bull-jean back to breathing

but as bull-jean rise stand in yard

seem like i float away

up up up further further further away

as ole caney sharp and crunch to get to tapping they canes

tapping tapping they canes louder louder faster faster

they tapping take me up and further away as

bull-jean stand in she yard looking up

breathing

tears rushing down both sides she face

bull-jean get to breathing faster

tears rush harder

ole caney sharp and crunch tapping they tapping they tapping faster till

bam

on ground on grass in front of bull-jean and mina house

bull-jean pass out

again

and the sky blink

carry me away

**1.**

*Love is all there Is.*

**1.**

shiny run out go house to house
stomping dusting da road shouting
great big mamma say come by
great big mamma say come by
great big mamma say come by

the peoples come quick pouring out

bull-jean
big bill and da family
stacks
and stacks dog queen
all head out bull-jean and mina house
cross she yard through gate
to middle the road.

all the children who mina done passed she fan making on to
come running and laughing and skipping and fanning and tumbling
out stacks lil ole shack back of bull-jean and mina house
cross the yard
through bull-jean and mina back door

out the front door
off the porch
cross the yard
pass the gate
and spill into middle the road
running in all directions up and down and back
shaking the air with the colors of they fans
and sounds that tickle.

mina
doctor black
bull-jean son-man
bull-jean son-man boy-child jr
and great big mamma
walk out
stepping side to side
till they get center
middle the road.
great big mamma then look up.
breathe.

great big mamma nodd to snacks
who grab stacks hand
walk she center of all.
stacks in white shirt white pants white shoes
and shaved head
look up.
breathe.

bull-jean
big bill and da family
get to humming soft and sweet.
great big mamma lay she hands out
hands so large they brush the clouds
great big mamma with large hands
raise them towards stacks
sing songs with words
we ain't never heard
but understand.

ole caney sharp and crunch over there
get to drumming each they porch with they canes and moans.
we know what is ours to do now

we move right
clap
we turn left
raise our hands
with great big mamma brush the clouds
we move left
clap clap
we turn right
raise our hands
with great big mamma brush the clouds
clap clap clap
we move side to side
raise our hands

with great big mamma brush the clouds

bees join up
butterflies swarm
trees sway
birds get loud
great big mamma nodd she head
bull-jean step in front da family
raise and open she arms
big bill slowly release all the notes she been holding inside
bull-jean let loose she arms up down side ways circle open open open
she arms set loose da family sing a lifting to big bill notes released
which now falling falling falling everywhere.
ole caney sharp and crunch drum they porches with they canes faster.
snacks catch a wail
mina stand side of stacks speaking spanish
as she wave her hands high and all around where stacks stand
great big mamma move to back of stacks
with large hands raised brush the clouds swirl and surround stacks

bull-jean son-man boy-child jr step front of stacks stare
stand still stare into stacks
fanning he eyelashes that seem to reach and curl the sun
back into the light of his light light eyes
bringing all them that was
and all coming
swimming round he head
looking at stacks through he eyes

lil bits
he body curved like a flowing river
walk through join center the middle the road
which cause folk to get to falling out
cause they soul know what coming
but they Spirit ain't grow'd enough to hold on to it
mean time

all the children who mina done passed she fan making on to come
running and laughing and skipping and fanning and tumbling
middle the road in all directions up and down and back
shaking the air with sounds that tickle
and fans swirling colors brighter and brighter so bright till we have to
close our eyes
just as lil bits open he mouth
get inside big bill and da family's notes
send he own
so filled with glory
that everything open in its presence.

stacks dog queen get to running in circles
middle the road up and down
tongue hanging out she head
she spin and spin and spin and run some more
ole caney sharp and crunch drumming they canes
bull-jean son-man boy-child jr with he fan and eyelashes
bull-jean loosed arms
big mamma swirling clouds

mina side of stacks
the bees
the trees
the butterflies
the birds
da family
big bill
the children laughing and running and tumbling and fanning
get louder
all the while
lil bits notes coming down pierce glory
through the top of we heads
likc lightning hit and burn
lil bits spin he notes in all directions louder faster higher
grace step through join in
till we feel something raining down on us

we open our eyes we see
we see dat black mermaid man lady with fishes and fishes and pearls
flowing all the way down past behind brush the clouds
ga ga ga    ga ga ga    ga ga ga
and all the children mina done passed she fan making on to
throw they fans into the now opened sky
and a hush descend down upon us cascading
calla lilies orchids tulips jasmines peonies azaleas daffodils geraniums
irises chrysanthemum sun flowers and more

we all fall to the fresh petal covered earth.

except stacks
and great big mamma
and bull-jean son-man boy-child jr
and stacks dog queen
they stand there
looking up
to the flowered opened sky
breathing in
the new day

paved with tears

*Then See*
*what had happened was*
*all turn*
*look my way*

*and the churning in bull-jean's heart reached me and I knew why*
*all the circling and telling and opening and praying and dreaming*
*had been swirling and coming back and moving through and falling out*
*and around*
*and right then in the flicker of that*
*I saw bull-jean son-man boy-child jr*
*fly straight into bull-jean's heart*
*into the churning*
*with he eyelashes*
*that seem to reach and curl the sun*
*back into the light of his light light eyes*
*he long long black hair*

*pull tightly into the black black of he skin*
*which paint a powerful picture*
*of all them that was*
*and they pull me in too*
*straight into bull-jean's heart*
*into the churning*
*and we fly.*

*and I know what was mines to do*
*to offer back*
*to grow through*
*to return*
*and Lift we.*

*and I cried*
*and I cried*
*and my tears woke me*
*and carried me in their flood*
*washing me in*
*every never earthed dream*
*all the broken promises*
*the thickened scars*
*and ruptured hands*
*the years of dancing on shards of regret and shame*
*with dampened desires*
*and snuffled out light*
*the pretending*
*the turned away*

*the smoothed over*

*the act like*

*the fester*

*the put on*

*the tight lips*

*the half open eyes*

*the hushed spirit*

*the pushed away truth*

*the heavy*

*the drowned.*

*and I knew*

*I was born for this*

*to Love*

*what is possible*

*to Life*

and they rose

up up up

they rose

smiling smiling smiling

ga ga ga    ga ga ga    ga ga ga

running and laughing and skipping and fanning and tumbling

flick wave circle drop clap twirl

play call pray

flick wave circle drop clap twirl play call pray

they rose

waving smiling

never leaving
they rose
carrying me to you

## 1.

*May all the courage that you have so desperately walked with*
*circle back and strengthen your next steps*

*May every act of self-determination that you have enacted*
*return as Divine defiance Lighting your Way*

*May all the laughter that you have poured into gatherings*
*spill back into your bones and move you to dance*

*May your unrequited curiosities*
*your deep down dreams*
*every bit of never returned love*
*each yearning*
*all your longings*
*may they show themselves to you*
*unfurrowed*
*and loosed in Light*

*May regret and grief and shame ungrip your Spirit*

*May you be healed in all directions of time*

*May you break the bondage of cycles that cause harm*

*May you Soar in new possibilities*

*May the Stars blanket your return within and beyond the veils*

*May Love become you*

*May you welcome*
*walk with*
*and Witness*
*those coming*

*May you be Free*

*Remember.*

**34.**

we wake

## closing | signe v. harriday

*Fire*      *FireFireFire*

*Water*      *WaterWaterWater*

*Word*      *WordWordWord*

*Wind*

*Wind*      *WindWind*

*Song*      *SongSongSong*

As a daughter of a pastor perhaps it's no wonder that ritual emerges in my artistry and magnetizes me toward artists who are grounded in a ritual praxis. As a little girl, sung liturgy was both salve and sacrament as I sat on wooden pews attuned to stories meant to stir the soul. The church was where I first met art and her fire. She was everywhere. In the stoles, the candles, the music, the storytelling, the altars, the lecterns, the pulpits, the flowers, the symbolism, the grandeur, the preparation before the event, the ritual, the public funding, and the ascension to other worlds, all while gathering in community. I remember slipping off my shoes, sliding next to my grandmother on the oversized bench, and letting my feet dangle above the massive pedals of the church organ. I remember carefully robing in red cassocks with white yokes to perform my duties as an acolyte. Standing before the congregation to deliver song or script were my first experiences with public performance. And at its core, through my father's voice, church was/is about learning to walk through the world more principled and oriented to care. Rituals offer space for the body and spirit to merge, vibrating us toward healing. My father wasn't my only ancestor called to ministry. So I figure some of what makes me the artist I am comes from seeds planted and watered by unsuspecting ancestors. Like the scattered seeds from an unlabeled package in the spring, I don't think they could have imagined I would be the harvest that sprung up from their hopes. I nonetheless see my work in their lineage.

The theater can be a living, breathing praxis in healing, a necessary ritual. I want to weave my lived lessons, cultural inheritances, and creativity into story tapestries that are evocative and purposeful. And as I grow, I feel myself ever drawn to artists that call me home with their ritual intuition and location. Sharon Bridgforth, with her uncompromising brilliance, conjures rituals that transport and transform us all.

Sharon's writing feels like church to me. The aliveness of her characters and texts compels us to elevate and go deeper at the same time. I remember the first time I heard Sharon's words. They transported me to a world I'd only dreamt about in whispers and glimpses. A world I could touch no more than I could contain the wind. It was the late '90s and I was piecing together my own Black lesbian quilt for support and sustenance (insert euphemism). Looking for connections and home—and we was doin' it. But I hadn't in all my wildest dreams imagined or known the voices of aunties or sapphic ancestors. Enter bull-jean, swaggering and sauntering into my mind bringing all the afro-mation my roots needed. These herstories nurtured me and invigorated my spirit. They connected me to a past I didn't know and helped me to unfurl into my own knowingness. Holding *the bull-jean stories* in my hands felt like holding a family scrapbook. And for more than 20 years since, I have returned to these sacred stories that are themselves the composition of a ritual.

And though I may have hoped, I hadn't imagined that Sharon would bring another incarnation for bull-jean into our world. Enter *bull-jean/ we wake*. Talk about deliverance!

Like wind chimes improvising melodic scores, the words of *bull-jean/we wake* murmur spells and stories that are enchanting. Sharon once again invites the specificity of repetition and the expansiveness of rhythm on the page to create a liminal prayer space for both the familiar and ethereal. Riding the waves of grief, Sharon lets me listen to these songs like I listened to the liturgy. The listening beckons me to discover sorrow wrapped in joy, longing veiled in memory, and a cast of family relations vacillating their own rooted and unrootedness. The journey echoes truths that remind us of the knowingness of children and elders, the awesome power of community, and the enduring power of love. I find ways of being through the voices and I find myself closer to healed, closer to my beloveds who have passed, closer to myself.

Communion will happen in the circles these texts will form. In those circles I can imagine how we will be called to witness and testify about our own remembering as we make rituals that bring us closer together.

*Wind*   *Word*   *Water*Fire

*Song*

– Signe V. Harriday

## contributors

**Sharon Bridgforth** (she/her/Mermaid) is a writer that creates ritual/jazz theater. A 2022 winner of Yale's Windham Campbell Prize in Drama, Sharon is a 2020-2023 Playwrights' Center Core Member, a 2022-2023 McKnight Fellow, and a New Dramatists alum. She has received support from the Doris Duke Performing Artist Award, Creative Capital, MAP Fund and the National Performance Network. Her writing is featured in *Teaching Black: The Craft of Teaching on Black Life and Literature*; *Mouths of Rain: An Anthology of Black Lesbian Thought,* and Feminist Studies' special issue commemorating 40 years of *This Bridge Called My Back* and *But Some of Us Are Brave!* Sharon's *dat Black Mermaid Man Lady/The Show* is streaming on the Twin Cities' PBS platform.

**Mary Anne Adams**—An activist/organizer, community public health researcher, and social worker, Mary Anne Adams earned a master's degree in Social Work from Georgia State University and has done extensive work in LGBT health. She is the founder and executive director of ZAMI NOBLA-National Organization of Black Lesbians on Aging, dedicated to building a base of power for Black lesbians. She is currently co-investigator on a ground-breaking study assessing the impact of COVID-19 on the needs of aging lesbians. She serves as Commissioner and Board Chair with the East Point Housing Authority and on the LGBTQ Advisory Board to Atlanta Mayor Andre Dickens.

**Virginia Grise** is a recipient of the Alpert Award in the Arts, the Yale Drama Award, the Whiting Writers' Award, and the Princess Grace Award in Theater Directing. Her published work includes *Your Healing is Killing Me, blu* and *The Panza Monologues*. In addition to plays, she has created a body of work that is interdisciplinary and includes multimedia performance, dance theater, performance installations, guerilla theater, site specific interventions, and community gatherings. She holds an MFA in Writing for Performance from the California Institute of the

Arts and is the Mellon Foundation Playwright in Residence at Cara Mía Theatre in Dallas, Texas.

**Signe V. Harriday** (she/her) is a fierce visionary and powerful storyteller who crafts theater that awakens our individual and collective humanity. As a director, multidisciplinary artist, activist/abolitionist, facilitator, and producer, she uses theater as a catalyst to ask questions about who we are and who we are in relation to others. She is the Artistic Producing Director of Pillsbury House + Theatre, a center for creativity and community in Minneapolis. She is a founding member of Million Artist Movement, a network of artists and activists committed to Black liberation and healing. She's also a member of Rootsprings Cooperative cultivating healing space for BIPOC artists/activists/healers in MN. She is a Drama League Directing Fellow and earned her MFA in Acting at the Institute for Advanced Theatre Training at the American Repertory Theatre at Harvard and Moscow Art Theatre. She's also a gold medalist with her synchronized swimming team the Subversive Sirens. www.signeharriday.com

**Celeste Henery** is a cultural anthropologist working at the intersections of race, gender, and health. Dr. Henery's broader research interests include black ecologies, feminisms, diaspora studies, and death and dying. She currently works as a Research Associate in the Department of African and African Diaspora Studies at The University of Texas at Austin. Her writing on black life across the diaspora has been published in various academic journals and blogs, including *Black Perspectives*. In addition to her academic endeavors, Dr. Henery works as a mitigation specialist, conducts interviews for the Texas After Violence Project, and guides others in their creative lives.

## ABOUT THE PRESS

53rd State Press publishes lucid, challenging, and lively new writing for performance. Our catalog includes new plays as well as scores and notations for interdisciplinary performance, graphic adaptations, and essays on theater and dance.

53rd State Press was founded in 2007 by Karinne Keithley in response to the bounty of new writing in the downtown New York community that was not available except in the occasional reading or short-lived performance. In 2010, Antje Oegel joined her as a co-editor. In 2017, Kate Kremer took on the leadership of the volunteer editorial collective. For more information or to order books, please visit 53rdstatepress.org.

53rd State Press books are represented to the trade by TCG (Theatre Communications Group). TCG books are exclusively distributed to the book trade by Consortium Book Sales and Distribution, an Ingram Brand.


## LAND & LABOR ACKNOWLEDGMENTS

53rd State Press recognizes that much of the work we publish was first developed and performed on the unceded lands of the Lenape and Canarsie communities. Our books are stored on and shipped from the unceded lands of the Chickasaw, Cherokee, Shawnee, and Yuchi communities. The work that we do draws on natural resources that members of the Indigenous Diaspora have led the way in protecting and caretaking. We are grateful to these Indigenous communities, and commit to supporting Indigenous-led movements working to undo the harms of colonization.

As a press devoted to preserving the ephemeral experiments of the contemporary avant-garde, we recognize with great reverence the work of radical BIPOC artists whose (often uncompensated) experiments have been subject to erasure, appropriation, marginalization, and theft. We commit to amplifying the revolutionary experiments of earlier generations of BIPOC theatermakers, and to publishing, promoting, celebrating, and compensating the BIPOC playwrights and performers revolutionizing the field today.

*Particle + Wave: A Conversation* // Daniel Alexander Jones + Alexis Pauline Gumbs
*ASTRS* // Karinne Keithley Syers
*The Lost Conversation: Interviews with an Enduring Avant-Garde* // Sara Farrington
*I Understand Everything Better* // David Neumann/Advanced Beginner Group
*uncollected trash collection* // Kate Kremer
*bull-jean & dem/dey back* // Sharon Bridgforth

FORTHCOMING

*SKiNFOLK: An American Show* // Jillian Walker
*The Securely Conferred, Vouchsafed Keepsakes of Maery S.* // Sibyl Kempson
*Angela's Mixtape + The History of Light* // Eisa Davis
*Sharon Bridgforth + Daniel Alexander Jones: A Conversation* // Sharon Bridgforth + Daniel Alexander Jones
*Ramp + Mushroom* // Eisa Davis
*Two Conversations* // Eisa Davis + Jillian Walker
*Wood Calls Out to Wood* // Corinne Donly
*The Incomplete Amber Reed* // Amber Reed
*Karen Davis: Bitter Pill, Mistook Acerbic for Advil* // Jess Barbagallo
*Broken Clothing* // Suzanne Bocanegra

*bull-jean & dem/dey back* is made possible by the New York State Council on the Arts with the support of the Office of the Governor and the New York State Legislature.

NEW YORK STATE OF OPPORTUNITY. | **Council on the Arts**

53rd State Press
new writing for performance

*The Book of the Dog* // Karinne Keithley
*Joyce Cho Plays* // Joyce Cho
*No Dice* // Nature Theater of Oklahoma
*When You Rise Up* // Miguel Gutierrez
*Montgomery Park, or Opulence* // Karinne Keithley
*Crime or Emergency* // Sibyl Kempson
*Off the Hozzle* // Rob Erickson
*A Map of Virtue + Black Cat Lost* // Erin Courtney
*Pig Iron: Three Plays* // Pig Iron Theatre Company
*The Mayor of Baltimore + Anthem* // Kristen Kosmas
*Ich, Kürbisgeist + The Secret Death of Puppets* // Sibyl Kempson
*Soulographie: Our Genocides* // Erik Ehn
*Life and Times: Episode 1* // Nature Theater of Oklahoma
*Life and Times: Episode 2* // Nature Theater of Oklahoma
*Life and Times: Episode 3 + 4* // Nature Theater of Oklahoma
*The 53rd State Occasional No. 1* // Ed. Paul Lazar
*There There* // Kristen Kosmas
*Seagull (Thinking of You)* // Tina Satter
*Self Made Man Man Made Land* // Ursula Eagly
*Another Telepathic Thing* // Big Dance Theater
*Another Tree Dance* // Karinne Keithley Syers
*Let Us Now Praise Susan Sontag* // Sibyl Kempson
*Dance by Letter* // Annie-B Parson
*Pop Star Series* // Neal Medlyn
*The Javier Plays* // Carlos Murillo
*Minor Theater: Three Plays* // Julia Jarcho
*Ghost Rings* (12-inch vinyl) // Half Straddle
*A New Practical Guide to Rhetorical Gesture and Action* // NTU.S.A
*A Field Guide to iLANDing* // iLAND
*The 53rd State Occasional No. 2* // Ed. Will Arbery
*Suicide Forest* // Haruna Lee
*Rude Mechs' Lipstick Traces* // Lana Lesley + the Rude Mechs
*MILTON* // PearlDamour
*The People's Republic of Valerie, Living Room Edition* // Kristen Kosmas
*A Discourse on Method* // David Levine + Shonni Enelow
*Severed* // Ignacio Lopez
*Ann, Fran, and Mary Ann* // Erin Courtney
*Love Like Light* // Daniel Alexander Jones